Itty Bitty Animals™

General Information

Many of the products used in this pattern book can be purchased from local craft, fabric and variety stores, or from the Annie's Attic Needlecraft Catalog (see Customer Service information on page 48).

Contents

2 Itty Bitty Giraffe

5 Itty Bitty Puppy

8 Itty Bitty Crocodile

10 Itty Bitty Piggy

12 Itty Bitty Kitty

15 Itty Bitty Reindeer

18 Itty Bitty Bunny

21 Itty Bitty Monkey

23 Itty Bitty Elephant

26 Itty Bitty Panda

29 Itty Bitty Ballerina Bear

32 Itty Bitty Baby Bear

35 Itty Bitty Chef Bear

39 Itty Bitty Uncle Sam

43 Itty Bitty Santa Bear

47 Stitch Guide

48 Metric Conversion Charts

Itty Bitty **Giraffe**

SKILL LEVEL

INTERMEDIATE

FINISHED SIZE
4 inches tall

MATERIALS
- Aunt Lydia's Classic Crochet
  size 10 crochet cotton
  (350 yds per ball):
  1 ball #423 maize
  50 yds #131 fudge brown
  25 yds each #0310 copper mist
  and #12 black
- Size 7/1.65mm steel crochet hook
  or size needed to obtain gauge
- Tapestry needle
- Fiberfill
- Stitch marker

GAUGE
9 sc = 1 inch

PATTERN NOTES
Work in continuous rounds, do not turn
or join unless otherwise stated.

Mark first stitch of each round.

Join with slip stitch as indicated unless
otherwise stated.

SPECIAL STITCH
Cluster (cl): Holding back last lp of each st
on hook, 3 dc in place indicated, yo, pull
through all lps on hook.

INSTRUCTIONS
GIRAFFE
HEAD
Rnd 1: Beg at top, with maize, ch 2, 6 sc in 2nd ch
from hook, **do not join** (see Pattern Notes). (6 sc)

Rnd 2: 2 sc in each st around. (12 sc)

Rnd 3: [Sc in each of next 2 sts, 2 sc in next st]
around. (16 sc)

Rnd 4: [Sc in each of next 3 sts, 2 sc in next st]
around. (20 sc)

Rnd 5: [2 sc in next st, sc in each of next 4 sts]
around. (24 sc)

Rnds 6–11: Sc in each st around. At end of last
rnd, stuff Head.

Rnd 12: [Sc in each of next 4 sts, **sc dec** (see
Stitch Guide) in next 2 sts] around. (20 sc)

Rnd 13: [Sc dec in next 2 sts] around, **join** (see
Pattern Notes) in beg sc. Leaving 12-inch end,
fasten off.

BODY
Rnds 1–5: Rep rnds 1–5 of Head. *(24 sc)*

Rnds 6–15: Sc in each st around.

Rnd 16: [Sc in each of next 2 sts, sc dec in next 2 sts] around. Stuff Body. *(18 sc)*

Rnd 17: [Sc in next st, sc dec in next 2 sts] around. *(12 sc)*

Rnd 18: [Sc dec in next 2 sts] around, join in beg sc. Leaving long end, fasten off.

With long end, weave through sts, pull to close. Secure end.

NECK
Rnd 1: Beg at top, with maize, ch 14, sl st in first ch to form ring, sc in each ch around, **do not join.** *(14 sc)*

Rnd 2: Sc in each st around.

Rnd 3: [Sc in each of next 6 sts, 2 sc in next st] around. *(16 sc)*

Rnd 4: Sc in each st around.

Rnd 5: [Sc in each of next 7 sts, 2 sc in next st] around. *(18 sc)*

Rnd 6: Sc in each st around.

Rnd 7: [Sc in each of next 5 sts, 2 sc in next st] around, join in beg sc. Leaving 12-inch end, fasten off. Stuff Neck.

Using 12-inch end, sew rnd 7 of Neck to Body.

Using 12-inch end, sew Head to rnd 1 of Neck.

SNOUT
Rnd 1: With maize, ch 2, 6 sc in 2nd ch from hook, **do not join.** *(6 sc)*

Rnd 2: 2 sc in each st around. *(12 sc)*

Rnd 3: [Sc in each of next 5 sts, 2 sc in next st] around. *(14 sc)*

Rnd 4: Sc in each st around.

Rnd 5: [Sc in each of next 6 sts, 2 sc in next st] around. *(16 sc)*

Rnd 6: [Sc in each of next 7 sts, 2 sc in next st] around, join in beg sc. Stuff Snout. Leaving 12-inch end, fasten off.

With 12-inch end, sew Snout to lower part of Head as shown in photo.

FINISHING
Using **satin stitch** *(see Fig. 1)*, with black, embroider eyes above Snout as shown in photo.

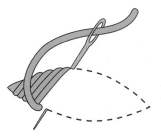

Fig. 1
Satin Stitch
(For Faces)

Using **straight stitch** *(see Fig. 2)*, with black, embroider 2 small sts for nostrils and V-shaped mouth as shown in photo.

Fig. 2
Straight Stitch

EAR
MAKE 2.
With maize, ch 5, sl st in 2nd ch from hook, sl st in next ch, sc in next ch, 2 hdc in last ch, working on opposite side of ch, 2 hdc in next ch, sc in next ch, sl st in each of last 2 chs. Leaving 8-inch end, fasten off.

Using 8-inch end, sew Ears to rnd 4 on Head as shown in photo.

LEG
MAKE 4.
Rnd 1: With fudge brown, ch 2, 7 sc in 2nd ch from hook, **do not join.** *(7 sc)*

Rnd 2: 2 sc in each st around. *(14 sc)*

Rnd 3: Sc in each st around, join in beg sc. Fasten off.

Rnd 4: Join maize with sc in first st, sc in each st around, do not join.

Rnds 5–14: Sc in each st around. At end of last rnd, join in beg sc. Leaving long end, fasten off.

FINISHING
Stuff Legs, using eraser end of pencil to push stuffing down.

Sew front Legs to Body, then sew inside of front Legs to each other along top 4 rnds so Legs don't splay out.

Rep for back Legs.

HORN
MAKE 2.
With fudge brown, ch 5, **cl** *(see Special Stitch)* in 3rd ch from hook, sl st in same ch, sl st in each of next 2 chs. Fasten off.

Sew Horns to top of Head as shown in photo.

MANE
With copper mist, ch 25, sl st in 2nd ch from hook, [ch 2, sl st in next ch] across to last ch, ch 2, sl st in last ch, working on opposite side of ch, sl st in next ch, [ch 2, sl st in next ch] across, ch 2, join in beg sl st. Leaving 18-inch end, fasten off.

Sew Mane to Head and Neck beg at rnd 3 of front of Head, down center back of Head and Neck as shown in photo.

TAIL
With maize, ch 7. Fasten off.

Cut 2 strands maize, each 4 inches long. Holding both strands tog, fold in half, pull fold part way through last ch, pull ends through fold. Pull to tighten.

Trim to 1 inch. Sew Tail to back of Body at top.

SPOTS
Using satin stitch, with copper mist, embroider markings randomly over Head, Neck and Body. ∎

Itty Bitty
Puppy

SKILL LEVEL

INTERMEDIATE

FINISHED SIZE
2½ inches tall

MATERIALS
- Aunt Lydia's Classic Crochet size 10 crochet cotton (350 yds per ball):
  1 ball #428 mint green
  50 yds #450 aqua
  25 yds #12 black
- Size 7/1.65mm steel crochet hook or size needed to obtain gauge
- Tapestry needle
- Fiberfill
- Stitch marker

GAUGE
9 sc = 1 inch

PATTERN NOTES
Work in continuous rounds, do not turn or join unless otherwise stated.

Mark first stitch of each round.

Join with slip stitch as indicated unless otherwise stated.

INSTRUCTIONS
PUPPY
HEAD
Rnd 1: With mint green, ch 2, 6 sc in 2nd ch from hook, **do not join** *(see Pattern Notes)*. *(6 sc)*

Rnd 2: 2 sc in each st around. *(12 sc)*

Rnd 3: [Sc in next st, 2 sc in next st] around. *(18 sc)*

Rnd 4: [Sc in each of next 2 sts, 2 sc in next st] around. *(24 sc)*

Rnd 5: [Sc in each of next 5 sts, 2 sc in next st] around. *(28 sc)*

Rnd 6: Sc in each st around.

Rnd 7: [Sc in each of next 13 sts, 2 sc in next st] around. *(30 sc)*

Rnds 8–13: Sc in each st around. At end of last rnd, stuff Head.

Rnd 14: [Sc in each of next 3 sts, **sc dec** (*see Stitch Guide*) in next 2 sts] around. (*24 sc*)

Rnd 15: [Sc in each of next 2 sts, sc dec in next 2 sts] around, **join** (*see Pattern Notes*) in beg sc. Fasten off.

BODY

Rnd 1: Beg at neck, with mint green, leaving 12-inch end, ch 18, sc in first ch to form ring, sc in each ch around, **do not join**. (*18 sc*)

Rnd 2: [Sc in each of next 5 sts, 2 sc in next st] around. (*21 sc*)

Rnd 3: Sc in each st around.

Rnd 4: [Sc in each of next 6 sts, 2 sc in next st] around. (*24 sc*)

Rnd 5: [Sc in each of next 3 sts, 2 sc in next st] around. (*30 sc*)

Rnds 6–12: Sc in each st around.

Rnd 13: [Sc in each of next 3 sts, sc dec in next 2 sts] around. (*24 sc*)

Rnd 14: [Sc in each of next 2 sts, sc dec in next 2 sts] around. (*18 sc*)

Rnd 15: [Sc dec in next 2 sts] around. (*9 sc*)

Rnd 16: [Sc dec in next 2 sts] 4 times, sl st in last st. Leaving long end, fasten off.

Stuff, using eraser end of pencil to push stuffing down.

Weave long end through top of sts on last rnd, pull to close. Secure end.

SNOUT

Rnds 1–3: With mint green, rep rnds 1–3 of Head. (*18 sc at end of last rnd*)

Rnds 4–6: Sc in each st around. At end of last rnd, join in beg sc. Leaving 10-inch end, fasten off.

Stuff, using eraser end of pencil to push stuffing down.

Using long end, sew Snout to lower part of Head as shown in photo.

FINISHING

Using **satin stitch** (*see Fig. 1*), with black, embroider eyes above Snout on Head and triangle-shaped nose on Snout as shown in photo.

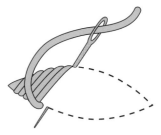

Fig. 1
Satin Stitch
(For Faces)

Using **straight stitch** (*see Fig. 2*), with black, embroider mouth under nose as shown in photo.

Fig. 2
Straight Stitch

EAR
MAKE 2.

Row 1: With aqua, ch 10, sc in 2nd ch from hook and in each of next 3 chs, hdc in each of next 3 chs, dc in next ch, 3 dc in last ch, working on opposite side of ch, 3 dc in next ch, dc in next ch, hdc in each of next 3 chs, sc in each of last 4 chs, turn. (*22 sts*)

Row 2: Ch 1, sl st in each of first 3 sts, sc in each of next 7 sts, 3 hdc in each of next 2 sts, sc in each of next 7 sts, sl st in each of last 3 sts. Leaving 8-inch end, fasten off.

Using long end, sew Ears to Head as shown in photo.

FRONT LEG
MAKE 2.

Rnd 1: Beg at top, with mint green, ch 12, sl st in first ch to form ring, sc in each ch around, **do not join**. (*12 sc*)

Rnds 2–11: Sc in each st around.

FOOT
Rnd 12: Sc in each of first 4 sts, 2 sc in each of next 4 sts, sc in each of last 4 sts. *(16 sc)*

Rnds 13–15: Sc in each st around.

Rnd 16: [Sc in each of next 2 sts, sc dec in next 2 sts] around. *(12 sc)*

Rnd 17: [Sc dec in next 2 sts] around, join in beg sc. Leaving long end, fasten off. *(6 sc)*

Weave long end through top of sts, pull to close. Secure end.

Stuff Leg, using eraser end of pencil to push stuffing down, leaving first 3 rnds at top unstuffed.

Flatten rnd 1 and sew top of Legs and rnds 1–5 of sides of Legs to Body at front as shown in photo.

BACK LEG
MAKE 2.
Rnd 1: Beg at haunch, with mint green, ch 2, 7 sc in 2nd ch from hook, **do not join.** *(7 sc)*

Rnd 2: 2 sc in each st around. *(14 sc)*

Rnds 3 & 4: Sc in each st around.

Rnd 5: [Sc in each of next 5 sts, sc dec in next 2 sts] around. *(12 sc)*

Rnds 6 & 7: Sc in each st around. Lightly stuff haunch section.

FOOT
Rnd 8: Sc in each of first 4 sts, 2 sc in each of next 4 sts, sc in each of last 4 sts. *(16 sc)*

Rnds 9–11: Sc in each st around.

Rnd 12: [Sc in each of next 2 sts, sc dec in next 2 sts] around. *(12 sc)*

Rnd 13: [Sc dec in next 2 sts] around, join in beg sc. Leaving long end, fasten off. *(6 sc)*

Weave long end through top of sts, pull to close. Secure end.

Sew rnds 1–4 of Legs to back of Body as shown in photo so Puppy is in sitting position.

TAIL
Rnd 1: Beg at tip, with mint green, ch 2, 6 sc in 2nd ch from hook, **do not join.** *(6 sc)*

Rnds 2 & 3: Sc in each st around.

Rnd 4: Sc in each of first 3 sts, 2 sc in next st, sc in each of last 2 sts. *(7 sc)*

Rnd 5: Sc in each st around.

Rnd 6: Sc in each of first 3 sts, 2 sc in next st, sc in each of last 3 sts. *(8 sc)*

Rnds 7 & 8: Sc in each st around.

Rnd 9: Hdc in each of first 4 sts, sl st in next st, leaving rem sts unworked. Leaving 8-inch end, fasten off.

Lightly stuff Tail.

Sew to bottom back of Body with hdc sts on bottom so Tail curves slightly upward. ∎

Itty Bitty Crocodile

SKILL LEVEL

INTERMEDIATE

FINISHED SIZE
4 inches long, including tail

MATERIALS
- Aunt Lydia's Classic Crochet size 10 crochet cotton (white: 400 yds per ball; solids: 350 yds per ball):
    1 ball #484 myrtle green
    25 yds each #12 black, #1 white and #422 golden yellow
- Size 7/1.65mm steel crochet hook or size needed to obtain gauge
- Tapestry needle
- Fiberfill
- Stitch marker

GAUGE
9 sc = 1 inch

PATTERN NOTES
Work in continuous rounds, do not turn or join unless otherwise stated.

Mark first stitch of each round.

Join with slip stitch as indicated unless otherwise stated.

INSTRUCTIONS
CROCODILE
HEAD & BODY
Rnd 1: Beg at snout, with myrtle green, ch 2, 6 sc in 2nd ch from hook, **do not join** (see Pattern Notes). (6 sc)

Rnd 2: 2 sc in each st around. (12 sc)

Rnds 3–6: Sc in each st around.

Rnd 7: Sc in each of first 4 sts, 2 sc in each of next 4 sts, sc in each of last 4 sts. (16 sc)

Rnds 8–10: Sc in each st around.

Rnd 11: Sc in each of first 6 sts, [**sc dec** (see Stitch Guide) in next 2 sts] 3 times, sc in each of last 4 sts. (13 sc)

Rnd 12: Sc in each of first 7 sts, sc dec in next 2 sts, sc in each of last 4 sts. Stuff snout and Head, using eraser end of pencil to push stuffing down. (12 sc)

Rnd 13: Sc in each st around.

Rnd 14: Sc in each of next 5 sts, *ch 9, sl st in 2nd ch from hook and in next ch, sc in each of next 2 chs, 3 hdc in next ch, hdc in each of next 3 chs (front leg)*, sc in same st as last sc, sc in each of next 5 sts, rep between * once, sc in each of last 2 sts.

Rnd 15: Sc in each of next 3 sts, 2 sc in next st, sc in next st, sk leg, sc in each of next 4 sts, 2 sc in next st, sk leg and sl st, sc in each of last 2 sts. (14 sc)

Rnd 16: Sc in each of first 6 sts, 2 sc in next st, sc in each of next 5 sts, 2 sc in next st, sc in last st. *(16 sc)*

Rnd 17: Sc in each of first 7 sts, 2 sc in next st, sc in each of next 6 sts, 2 sc in next st, sc in last st. Stuff Body and continue to stuff as you work.

Rnds 18–24: Sc in each st around.

Rnd 25: Sc in each of first 10 sts, leaving rem sts unworked. Mark last st as end of rnd.

Rnd 26: *Ch 9, sl st in 2nd ch from hook and in next ch, sc in each of next 2 chs, 3 hdc in next ch, hdc in each of next 3 chs *(back leg)*, sl st in same st as last st on rnd 25, sc in each of next 7 sts, rep between * once, sl st in last st as last sc, sc in each of next 11 sts.

Rnd 27: Sk leg and sl st, [sc in next st, sc dec in next 2 sts] twice, sk leg, sc in next sl st, sc dec in next 2 sts, [sc in next st, sc dec in next 2 sts] 3 times. *(12 sc)*

Rnd 28: Sc in each st around.

Rnd 29: [Sc in each of next 2 sts, sc dec in next 2 sts] around. *(9 sc)*

Rnd 30: Sc in each st around.

Row 31: Now working in rows, fold last rnd tog, working through both thicknesses, sc in each st across, turn. *(4 sc)*

Row 32: Ch 1, sc dec in first 2 sts, sc in next st, 2 sc in last st, turn.

Row 33: Ch 1, 2 sc in first st, sc in next st, sc dec in last 2 sts, turn.

Row 34: Ch 1, sc dec in first 2 sts, sc in each of last 2 sts, turn. *(3 sc)*

Row 35: Sc dec in first 2 sts, sc last st, ch 9, turn.

Row 36: Sl st in 2nd ch from hook and in next ch, sc in each of next 2 chs, 3 hdc in next ch,

hdc in each of next 3 chs *(tail)*, sk next st on last row, sl st in next st, leave last st unworked. Fasten off.

MOUTH
With white, ch 13. Leaving long end, fasten off.

Sew to snout as shown in photo.

FINISHING
Using **satin stitch** *(see Fig. 1)*, with golden yellow, embroider horizontal eyes over rnd 7 of Head.

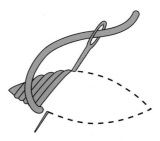

Fig. 1
Satin Stitch
(For Faces)

Using satin stitch, with black, embroider pupils with vertical sts on Eyes.

Using **French knot** *(see Fig. 2)*, with myrtle green, embroider nostrils between rnds 3 and 4 on Head as shown in photo.

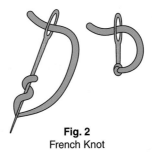

Fig. 2
French Knot

SPINE
With myrtle green, ch 24. Leaving long end, fasten off.

Sew Spine along center on top of Head and Body, beg at rnd 9 on Head and going back to row 34 at tail. ■

Itty Bitty Piggy

FINISHED SIZE
2¾ inches tall

MATERIALS
- Aunt Lydia's Classic Crochet size 10 crochet cotton (350 yds per ball):
  1 ball #424 light peach
  25 yds #12 black
- Size 7/1.65mm steel crochet hook or size needed to obtain gauge
- Tapestry needle
- Fiberfill
- Stitch marker

GAUGE
9 sc = 1 inch

PATTERN NOTES
Work in continuous rounds, do not turn or join unless otherwise stated.

Mark first stitch of each round.

Join with slip stitch as indicated unless otherwise stated.

INSTRUCTIONS
PIGGY
HEAD
Rnd 1: Beg at top, with light peach, ch 2, 6 sc in 2nd ch from hook, **do not join** (see Pattern Notes). (6 sc)

Rnd 2: 2 sc in each st around. (12 sc)

Rnd 3: [Sc in next st, 2 sc in next st] around. (18 sc)

Rnd 4: [Sc in each of next 2 sts, 2 sc in next st] around. (24 sc)

Rnd 5: [Sc in each of next 5 sts, 2 sc in next st] around. (28 sc)

Rnd 6: Sc in each st around.

Rnd 7: [Sc in each of next 13 sts, 2 sc in next st] around. (30 sc)

Rnds 8–13: Sc in each st around. At end of last rnd, stuff Head.

Rnd 14: [Sc in each of next 3 sts, **sc dec** (see Stitch Guide) in next 2 sts] around. (24 sc)

Rnd 15: [Sc in each of next 2 sts, sc dec in next 2 sts] around, **join** (see Pattern Notes) in beg sc. Leaving 12-inch end, fasten off. (18 sc)

BODY
Rnd 1: Beg at top, with light peach, ch 2, 6 sc in 2nd ch from hook, **do not join** (see Pattern Notes). (6 sc)

Rnd 2: 2 sc in each st around. (12 sc)

Rnd 3: [Sc in next st, 2 sc in next st] around. (18 sc)

Rnd 4: [Sc in each of next 2 sts, 2 sc in next st] around. (24 sc)

Rnd 5: [Sc in each of next 2 sts, 2 sc in next st] around. *(32 sc)*

Rnds 6–20: Sc in each st around. Stuff Body.

Rnd 21: [Sc in each of next 2 sts, sc dec in next 2 sts] around. *(24 sc)*

Rnd 22: [Sc in each of next 2 sts, sc dec in next 2 sts] around. *(18 sc)*

Rnd 23: [Sc in next st, sc dec in next 2 sts] around. *(12 sc)*

Finish stuffing Body.

Rnd 24: [Sc next 2 sts tog] around, join in beg sc. Leaving long end, fasten off. *(6 sc)*

Weave long end through top of sts of last rnd, pull to close. Secure end.

Using 12-inch end on Head, sew Head to Body as shown in photo.

SNOUT
Rnds 1 & 2: Rep rnds 1 and 2 of Body. *(12 sc at end of last rnd)*

Rnd 3: Working in **back lps** *(see Stitch Guide)*, sc in each st around, join in beg sc. Fasten off.

Stuff Snout.

Sew Snout to rnds 10–13 on Head as shown in photo.

FINISHING
Using **satin stitch** *(see Fig. 1)*, with black, embroider eyes above Snout as shown in photo.

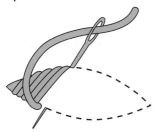

Fig. 1
Satin Stitch
(For Faces)

Using **straight stitch** *(see Fig. 2)*, with black, embroider 2 small vertical stitches on Snout for nostrils.

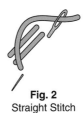

Fig. 2
Straight Stitch

EAR
MAKE 2.
Row 1: With light peach, ch 5, sc in 2nd ch from hook and in each ch across, turn. *(4 sc)*

Row 2: Ch 1, sc dec in first 2 sts, sc dec in last 2 sts, turn. *(2 sc)*

Row 3: Ch 1, sc dec in 2 sts. Fasten off. *(1 sc)*

EDGING
Join light peach with sc in end of row 1, sc in end of each of next 2 rows, 3 sc in next sc, sc in end of each row across to end. Fasten off.

Sew Ears to top of Head as shown in photo.

TAIL
With light peach, ch 7, 5 sc in 2nd ch from hook and in each ch across. Leaving 8-inch end, fasten off.

Using 8-inch end, sew Tail to back of Body at top.

LEG
MAKE 4.
Rnds 1–3: Rep rnds 1–3 of Body. *(18 sc at end of last rnd)*

Rnds 4–9: Sc in each st around. At end of last rnd, leaving 10-inch end, fasten off.

Stuff Legs.

Sew to bottom of Body as shown in photo. ∎

Itty Bitty
Kitty

SKILL LEVEL

INTERMEDIATE

FINISHED SIZE
2½ inches tall

MATERIALS
- Aunt Lydia's Classic Crochet size 10 crochet cotton (white: 400 yds per ball; solids: 350 yds per ball):
  1 ball #431 pumpkin
  50 yds #1 white
  25 yds each #12 black and
  #422 golden yellow
- Size 7/1.65mm steel crochet hook or size needed to obtain gauge
- Tapestry needle
- Fiberfill
- Stitch marker

GAUGE
9 sc = 1 inch

PATTERN NOTES
Work in continuous rounds, do not turn or join unless otherwise stated.

Mark first stitch of each round.

Join with slip stitch as indicated unless otherwise stated.

INSTRUCTIONS
KITTY
HEAD
Rnd 1: Beg at top, with pumpkin, ch 2, 6 sc in 2nd ch from hook, **do not join** (see Pattern Notes). (6 sc)

Rnd 2: 2 sc in each st around. (12 sc)

Rnd 3: [Sc in next st, 2 sc in next st] around. (18 sc)

Rnd 4: [Sc in each of next 2 sts, 2 sc in next st] around. (24 sc)

Rnd 5: [Sc in each of next 5 sts, 2 sc in next st] around. (28 sc)

Rnd 6: Sc in each st around.

Rnd 7: [Sc in each of next 13 sts, 2 sc in next st] around. (30 sc)

Rnds 8–13: Sc in each st around. At end of last rnd, stuff Head.

Rnd 14: [Sc in each of next 3 sts, **sc dec** (see Stitch Guide)] around. (24 sc)

Rnd 15: [Sc in each of next 2 sts, sc dec in next 2 sts] around, **join** (see Pattern Notes) in beg sc. Leaving 12-inch end, fasten off. (18 sc)

Stuff Head completely.

BODY
Rnd 1: Beg at neck, with pumpkin, leaving 12-inch end, ch 18, sl st in first ch to form ring, sc in each ch around, **do not join**. (18 sc)

Rnd 2: [Sc in each of next 5 sts, 2 sc in next st] around. *(21 sc)*

Rnd 3: Sc in each st around.

Rnd 4: [Sc in each of next 6 sts, 2 sc in next st] around. *(24 sc)*

Rnd 5: [Sc in each of next 3 sts, 2 sc in next st] around. *(30 sc)*

Rnds 6–12: Sc in each st around.

Rnd 13: [Sc in each of next 3 sts, sc dec in next 2 sts] around. *(24 sc)*

Rnd 14: [Sc in each of next 2 sts, sc dec in next 2 sts] around. *(18 sc)*

Rnd 15: [Sc dec in next 2 sts] around. *(9 sc)*

Rnd 16: [Sc dec in next 2 sts] 4 times, sl st in last st. Leaving long end, fasten off.

Stuff Body.

Weave long end through sts of last rnd, pull to close. Secure end.

Using 12-inch end, sew Head to Body as shown in photo.

SNOUT
Rnd 1: Beg at top, with white, ch 2, 6 sc in 2nd ch from hook, **do not join.** *(6 sc)*

Rnd 2: [Sc in next st, (sc, hdc, sc) in next st, 2 hdc in next st] around. *(12 sts)*

Rnd 3: [Sc in next st, 2 sc in next st, 3 hdc in next st, sc in each of next 2 sts, 3 sc in next st] around. *(22 sc)*

Rnd 4: Sc in each st around.

Row 5: Now working in rows, ch 1, sc in each of first 2 sts, leaving rem sts unworked, turn. *(2 sc)*

Row 6: Sc dec in next 2 sts. Leaving 12-inch end, fasten off.

Sew Snout to Head with row 6 at top, stuffing as you sew.

FINISHING
Using **satin stitch** *(see Fig. 1)*, with golden yellow, embroider horizontal eyes on rnds 7 and 8 of Head on each side of Snout as shown in photo.

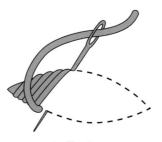

Fig. 1
Satin Stitch
(For Faces)

Using satin stitch, with black, embroider vertical pupils on eyes.

Using satin stitch, with black, embroider triangle-shaped nose on Snout as shown in photo.

Using **straight stitch** *(see Fig. 2)*, with black, embroider mouth as shown in photo.

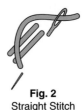

Fig. 2
Straight Stitch

WHISKERS
Cut 4 lengths of white, each 3½ inches long. Thread lengths through sts at either side of Snout. On 1 side, [tie 2 strands of white tog] twice.

Rep on other side.

Trim to desired length.

EAR
MAKE 2.
Row 1: With white, ch 5, sc in 2nd ch from hook and in each ch across, turn. *(4 sc)*

Row 2: Ch 1, sc dec in first 2 sts, sc dec in last 2 sts, turn. *(2 sc)*

Row 3: Ch 1, sc dec in next 2 sts. Fasten off. This is tip of Ear.

EDGING
Working around outer edge in ends of rows, join pumpkin with sc in end of row 1, sc in end of each row across to tip, 3 sc in tip, sc in end of each row across. Fasten off.

Sew Ears to top of Head as shown in photo.

TUMMY PANEL
Row 1: With white, ch 3, sc in 2nd ch from hook and in last ch, turn. *(2 sc)*

Row 2: Ch 1, 2 sc in first st, sc in last st, turn. *(3 sc)*

Row 3: 2 sc in first st, sc in each of last 2 sts, turn. *(4 sc)*

Row 4: 2 sc in first st, sc in each of next 2 sts, 2 sc in last st, turn. *(6 sc)*

Rows 5–9: Ch 1, sc in each st across, turn.

Row 10: Ch 1, sc dec in first 2 sts, sc in each of next 2 sts, sc dec in last 2 sts, turn. *(4 sc)*

Row 11: Ch 1, sc dec in first 2 sts, sc dec in last 2 sts, turn. Leaving 14-inch end, fasten off. *(2 sc)*

Sew Tummy Panel to front of Body as shown in photo.

FRONT LEG
MAKE 2.
Rnd 1: Beg at top, with pumpkin, leaving 12-inch end, ch 12, sl st in first ch to form ring, sc in each ch around, **do not join.** *(12 sc)*

Rnds 2–11: Sc in each st around. At end of last rnd, join in beg sc. Fasten off.

Rnd 12: Beg at foot, join white with sc in first st, sc in each of next 3 sts, 2 sc in each of next 4 sts, sc in each of last 4 sts. *(16 sc)*

Rnds 13–15: Sc in each st around.

Rnd 16: [Sc in each of next 2 sts, sc dec in next 2 sts] around. *(12 sc)*

Rnd 17: [Sc dec in next 2 sts] around, join in beg sc. Leaving long end, fasten off.

Using long end, weave through top of sts on last rnd, pull to close. Secure end.

Stuff Leg, using eraser end of pencil to push stuffing down, leaving top 3 rnds unstuffed.

Flatten first rnd and sew closed.

Sew to each side of Body below Head as shown in photo.

BACK LEG
MAKE 2.
Rnd 1: Starting at haunch section with pumpkin, ch 2, 7 sc in 2nd ch from hook, **do not join.** *(7 sc)*

Rnd 2: 2 sc in each st around. *(14 sc)*

Rnds 3 & 4: Sc in each st around.

Rnd 5: [Sc in each of next 5 sts, sc dec in next 2 sts] around. *(12 sc)*

Rnds 6 & 7: Sc in each st around. At end of last rnd, join in beg sc. Fasten off.

Lightly stuff haunch.

Rnds 8–13: Rep rnds 12–17 of Front Leg, stuffing as you work.

Sew rnds 1–4 of Legs to Body as shown in photo so Kitty is in sitting position.

TAIL
Row 1: With pumpkin, ch 14, hdc in 3rd ch from hook, hdc in each ch across, turn.

Row 2: Ch 1, sc in each st across, turn.

Row 3: Fold in half lengthwise, working through both thicknesses, sl st in each st across. Fasten off.

Sew 1 end of Tail to back of Body at top. ∎

Itty Bitty
Reindeer

SKILL LEVEL

INTERMEDIATE

FINISHED SIZE
3½ inches tall, including antlers

MATERIALS
- Aunt Lydia's Classic Crochet size 10 crochet cotton (350 yds per ball):
  1 ball #0310 copper mist
  50 yds #420 cream
  25 yds each #12 black and #494 victory red
- Size 7/1.65mm steel crochet hook or size needed to obtain gauge
- Tapestry needle
- ½-inch wide plaid ribbon: 10 inches
- Fiberfill
- Stitch marker

GAUGE
9 sc = 1 inch

PATTERN NOTES
Work in continuous rounds, do not turn or join unless otherwise stated.

Mark first stitch of each round.

Join with slip stitch as indicated unless otherwise stated.

SPECIAL STITCH
Cluster (cl): Holding back last lp of each st on hook, 3 dc in place indicated, yo, pull though all lps on hook.

INSTRUCTIONS
REINDEER
HEAD
Rnd 1: Beg at top, with copper mist, ch 2, 6 sc in 2nd ch from hook, **do not join** (*see Pattern Notes*). (*6 sc*)

Rnd 2: 2 sc in each st around. (*12 sc*)

Rnd 3: [Sc in next st, 2 sc in next st] around. (*18 sc*)

Rnd 4: [Sc in each of next 2 sts, 2 sc in next st] around. (*24 sc*)

Rnd 5: [Sc in each of next 5 sts, 2 sc in next st] around. (*28 sc*)

Rnd 6: Sc in each st around.

Rnd 7: [Sc in each of next 13 sts, 2 sc in next st] around. (*30 sc*)

Rnds 8–13: Sc in each st around. At end of last rnd, stuff Head.

Rnd 14: [Sc in each of next 3 sts, **sc dec** *(see Stitch Guide)* in next 2 sts] around. *(24 sc)*

Rnd 15: [Sc in each of next 2 sts, sc dec in next 2 sts] around, **join** *(see Pattern Notes)* in beg sc. Leaving 12-inch end, fasten off. *(18 sc)*

Stuff Head completely.

BODY

Rnd 1: Beg at neck, with copper mist, ch 18, sl st in first ch to form ring, sc in each ch around, **do not join**. *(18 sc)*

Rnd 2: [Sc in each of next 5 sts, 2 sc in next st] around. *(21 sc)*

Rnd 3: Sc in each st around.

Rnd 4: [Sc in each of next 6 sts, 2 sc in next st] around. *(24 sc)*

Rnd 5: [Sc in each of next 3 sts, 2 sc in next st] around. *(30 sc)*

Rnds 6–12: Sc in each st around.

Rnd 13: [Sc in each of next 3 sts, sc dec in next 2 sts] around. *(24 sc)*

Rnd 14: [Sc in each of next 2 sts sc dec in next 2 sts] around. *(18 sc)*

Rnd 15: [Sc dec in next 2 sts] around. *(9 sc)*

Rnd 16: [Sc dec in next 2 sts] 4 times, sl st in last st. Leaving long end, fasten off.

Weave long end through top of sts on last rnd, pull to close. Secure end.

Stuff Body, using eraser end of pencil to push stuffing down.

Using 12-inch end, sew Head to Body.

SNOUT

Rnd 1: With cream, ch 2, 6 sc in 2nd ch from hook, **do not join**. *(6 sc)*

Rnd 2: 2 sc in each st around. *(12 sc)*

Rnd 3: [2 sc in each of next 3 sts, sc in each of next 3 sts] around. *(18 sc)*

Rnds 4–6: Sc in each st around. At end of last rnd, leaving 12-inch end, fasten off.

Stuff Snout and sew to lower part of Head.

NOSE

With victory red, ch 3, **cl** *(see Special Stitch)* in 3rd ch from hook, ch 1, sl st in same ch. Leaving 8-inch end, fasten off.

Sew Nose to Snout as shown in photo.

FINISHING

Using **satin stitch** *(see Fig. 1)*, with black, embroider eyes above Snout as shown in photo.

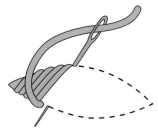

Fig. 1
Satin Stitch
(For Faces)

Using **straight stitch** *(see Fig. 2)*, with black, embroider mouth on Snout as shown in photo.

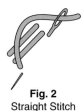

Fig. 2
Straight Stitch

EAR
MAKE 2.

With copper mist, ch 5, sl st in 2nd ch from hook and in next ch, sc in next ch, 2 hdc in last ch, working on opposite side of ch, 2 hdc in next ch, sc in next ch, sl st in each of last 2 chs. Leaving 8-inch end, fasten off.

Sew Ears to rnd 5 on Head as shown in photo.

ANTLER
MAKE 2.

With cream, ch 7, sc in 2nd ch from hook, (sc, ch 3, sc) in next ch, sk next ch, (sc, ch 2, 2 hdc in 2nd ch from hook, sc) in next ch, sk next ch, (sc, hdc, dc) in last ch, working on opposite side of ch, (dc, hdc, sc) in first ch, sl st in next ch, (sc, ch 3, sc) in next ch, sl st in each of last 3 chs. Leaving 10-inch end, fasten off.

Sew Antlers to top of Head between Ears as shown in photo.

FRONT LEG
MAKE 2.

Rnd 1: With copper mist, leaving 14-inch end, ch 12, sc in first ch to form ring, sc in each ch around, **do not join.** (*12 sc*)

Rnds 2–11: Sc in each st around.

Rnd 12: Beg at foot, sc in each of first 4 sts, 2 sc in each of next 4 sts, sc in each of last 4 sts. (*16 sc*)

Rnds 13–15: Sc in each st around.

Rnd 16: [Sc in each of next 2 sts, sc dec in next 2 sts] around. (*12 sc*)

Rnd 17: [Sc in next 2 sts] around, join in beg sc. Leaving long end, fasten off. (*6 sc*)

Weave long end through top of sts on last rnd, pull to close. Secure end.

Stuff Legs, using eraser end of pencil to push stuffing down, leaving first 3 rnds unstuffed.

Flatten rnd 1, sew closed.

Sew top of Legs to rnds 1–5 on front of Body below Head as shown in photo.

BACK LEG
MAKE 2.

Rnd 1: Beg at haunch, with copper mist, leaving 12-inch end, ch 2, 7 sc in 2nd ch from hook, **do not join.** (*7 sc*)

Rnd 2: 2 sc in each st around. (*14 sc*)

Rnds 3 & 4: Sc in each st around.

Rnd 5: [Sc in each of next 5 sts, sc dec in next 2 sts] around. (*12 sc*)

Rnds 6 & 7: Sc in each st around. Lightly stuff haunch.

Rnds 8–13: Rep rnds 12–17 of Front Leg, stuffing as you work.

Sew rnds 1–4 of Legs to Body as shown in photo so Reindeer is in sitting position.

Tie ribbon in bow around neck. ∎

Itty Bitty Bunny

SKILL LEVEL

INTERMEDIATE

FINISHED SIZE
3½ inches tall, including Ears

MATERIALS
- Aunt Lydia's Classic Crochet size 10 crochet cotton (white: 400 yds per ball; solids: 350 yds per ball):
    1 ball #1 white
    50 yds #401 orchid pink
    25 yds #12 black
- Size 7/1.65mm steel crochet hook or size needed to obtain gauge
- Tapestry needle
- Fiberfill
- Stitch marker

GAUGE
9 sc = 1 inch

PATTERN NOTES
Work in continuous rounds, do not turn or join unless otherwise stated.

Mark first stitch of each round.

Join with slip stitch as indicated unless otherwise stated.

SPECIAL STITCH
Cluster (cl): Holding back last lp of each st on hook, 3 dc in place indicated, yo, pull though all lps on hook.

INSTRUCTIONS
BUNNY
HEAD
Rnd 1: Beg at top, with white, ch 2, 6 sc in 2nd ch from hook, **do not join** (see Pattern Notes). (6 sc)

Rnd 2: 2 sc in each st around. (12 sc)

Rnd 3: [Sc in next st, 2 sc in next st] around. (18 sc)

Rnd 4: [Sc in each of next 2 sts, 2 sc in next st] around. (24 sc)

Rnd 5: [Sc in each of next 5 sts, 2 sc in next st] around. (28 sc)

Rnd 6: Sc in each st around.

Rnd 7: [Sc in each of next 13 sts, 2 sc in next st] around. (30 sc)

Rnds 8–13: Sc in each st around. At end of last rnd, stuff Head.

Rnd 14: [Sc in each of next 3 sts, **sc dec** *(see Stitch Guide)* in next 2 sts] around. *(24 sc)*

Rnd 15: [Sc in each of next 2 sts, sc dec in next 2 sts] around, **join** *(see Pattern Notes)* in beg sc. Leaving 12-inch end, fasten off. *(18 sc)*

Stuff Head completely.

BODY
Rnd 1: Beg at neck, with white, ch 18, sl st in first ch to form ring, sc in each ch around, **do not join.** *(18 sc)*

Rnd 2: [Sc in each of next 5 sts, 2 sc in next st] around. *(21 sc)*

Rnd 3: Sc in each st around.

Rnd 4: [Sc in each of next 6 sts, 2 sc in next st] around. *(24 sc)*

Rnd 5: [Sc in each of next 3 sts, 2 sc in next st] around. *(30 sc)*

Rnds 6–12: Sc in each st around.

Rnd 13: [Sc in each of next 3 sts, sc dec in next 2 sts] around. *(24 sc)*

Rnd 14: [Sc in each of next 2 sts sc dec in next 2 sts] around. *(18 sc)*

Rnd 15: [Sc dec in next 2 sts] around. *(9 sc)*

Rnd 16: [Sc dec in next 2 sts] 4 times, sl st in last st. Leaving long end, fasten off.

Weave long end through top of sts on last rnd, pull to close. Secure end.

Stuff Body, using eraser end of pencil to push stuffing down.

Using 12-inch end, sew Head to Body.

CHEEK
MAKE 2.
Rnds 1 & 2: Rep rnds 1 and 2 of Head. *(12 sc)*

Rnds 3 & 4: Sc in each st around. At end of last rnd, join in beg sc. Leaving 8-inch end, fasten off.

Stuff Cheeks.

Sew to lower part of Head as shown in photo.

NOSE
With orchid pink, ch 3, **cl** *(see Special Stitch)* in 3rd ch from hook, ch 1, sl st in same ch. Fasten off.

Sew Nose between Cheeks as shown in photo.

FINISHING
Using **satin stitch** *(see Fig. 1)*, with black, embroider eyes on Head above Cheeks as shown in photo.

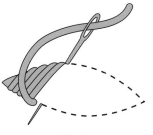

Fig. 1
Satin Stitch
(For Faces)

INNER EAR
MAKE 2.
With orchid pink, ch 10, sc in 2nd ch from hook and in each of next 3 chs, hdc in each of next 3 chs, dc in next ch, 3 dc in last ch, working on opposite side of ch, 3 dc in next ch, dc in next ch, hdc in each of next 3 chs, sc in each of last 4 chs. Fasten off.

OUTER EAR
MAKE 2.
Row 1: With white, ch 10, sc in 2nd ch from hook and in each of next 3 chs, hdc in each of next 3 chs, dc in next ch, 3 dc in last ch, working on opposite side of ch, 3 dc in next ch, dc in next ch, hdc in each of next 3 chs, sc in each of last 4 chs, turn.

Row 2: Holding 1 Inner Ear on top with WS tog, working through both thicknesses, ch 1, sc in each of first 10 sts, 2 sc in next st, ch 1, 2 sc in next st, sc in each of last 10 sts. Fasten off.

Sew Ears to top of Head as shown in photo.

LEG
MAKE 2.

Rnd 1: With white, ch 2, 6 sc in 2nd ch from hook. *(6 sc)*

Rnd 2: 2 sc in first st, sc in next st, 2 hdc in each of next 2 sts, sc in next st, 2 sc in last st. *(10 sts)*

Rnd 3: 2 sc in first st, sc in each of next 2 sts, 2 hdc in each of next 4 sts, sc in next st, 2 sc in next st, sc in last st. *(16 sts)*

Rnd 4: Sl st in next st, ch 1, working in **back lps** *(see Stitch Guide)*, sc in first st and in each st around.

Rnd 5: Sc in each of first 5 sts, [sc dec in next 2 sts] 3 times, sc in each of last 5 sts. *(13 sc)*

Rnd 6: Sc in each of first 5 sts, sc dec in next 2 sts, sc in each of last 6 sts. *(12 sc)*

Rnds 7 & 8: Sc in each st around.

Rnd 9: [Sc in each of next 2 sts, 2 sc in next st] around. *(16 sc)*

Rnd 10: [Sc in each of next 7 sts, 2 sc in next st] around, join in beg sc. Leaving 12-inch end, fasten off.

Stuff Legs.

Sew to front of Body as shown in photo so Bunny is in sitting position.

ARM
MAKE 2.

Rnd 1: Beg at top with white, leaving 10-inch end, ch 11, sc in first ch to form ring, sc in each ch around, **do not join.** *(11 sc)*

Rnds 2–6: Sc in each st around.

Rnd 7: Sc in each of first 4 sts, 2 sc in each of next 3 sts, sc in each of last 4 sts. *(14 sc)*

Rnds 8 & 9: Sc in each st around.

Rnd 10: [Sc in next st, sc dec in next 2 sts, sc in each of next 2 sts, sc dec in next 2 sts] around. *(10 sc)*

Rnd 11: [Sc dec in next 2 sts] around, join in beg sc. Leaving long end, fasten off. *(5 sc)*

Weave long end through top of sts of last rnd, pull to close. Secure end.

Stuff Arms, using eraser end of pencil to push stuffing down, leaving first 3 rnds unstuffed at top.

Flatten last rnd and sew closed.

Sew Arms to rnds 2–5 on Body, angled slightly towards back as shown in photo.

TAIL

Rnds 1 & 2: Rep rnds 1 and 2 of Head. *(12 sc)*

Rnds 3 & 4: Sc in each st around. At end of last rnd, join in beg sc. Leaving 8-inch end, fasten off.

Lightly stuff Tail and sew to bottom back of Body. ■

Itty Bitty Monkey

FINISHED SIZE
2½ inches tall

MATERIALS
- Aunt Lydia's Classic Crochet size 10 crochet cotton (350 yds per ball):
  1 ball #131 fudge brown
  50 yds #420 cream
  25 yds #12 black
- Size 7/1.65mm steel crochet hook or size needed to obtain gauge
- Tapestry needle
- Fiberfill
- Stitch marker

GAUGE
9 sc = 1 inch

PATTERN NOTES
Work in continuous rounds, do not turn or join unless otherwise stated.

Mark first stitch of each round.

Join with slip stitch as indicated unless otherwise stated.

INSTRUCTIONS
MONKEY
HEAD
Rnd 1: Beg at top, with fudge brown, ch 2, 6 sc in 2nd ch from hook, **do not join** (see Pattern Notes). (6 sc)

Rnd 2: 2 sc in each st around. (12 sc)

Rnd 3: [Sc in next st, 2 sc in next st] around. (18 sc)

Rnd 4: [Sc in each of next 2 sts, 2 sc in next st] around. (24 sc)

Rnd 5: [Sc in each of next 5 sts, 2 sc in next st] around. (28 sc)

Rnd 6: Sc in each st around.

Rnd 7: [Sc in each of next 13 sts, 2 sc in next st] around. (30 sc)

Rnds 8–13: Sc in each st around. At end of last rnd, stuff Head.

Rnd 14: [Sc in each of next 3 sts, **sc dec** (see Stitch Guide) in next 2 sts] around. (24 sc)

Rnd 15: [Sc in each of next 2 sts, sc dec in next 2 sts] around, **join** (see Pattern Notes) in beg sc. Leaving 12-inch end, fasten off. (18 sc)

Stuff Head completely.

BODY
Rnd 1: Beg at neck with fudge brown, ch 18, sc in first ch to form ring, sc in each ch around, **do not join.** (18 sc)

Rnd 2: [Sc in each of next 5 sts, 2 sc in next st] around. *(21 sc)*

Rnd 3: Sc in each st around.

Rnd 4: [Sc in each of next 6 sts, 2 sc in next st] around. *(24 sc)*

Rnd 5: [Sc in each of next 3 sts, 2 sc in next st] around. *(30 sc)*

Rnds 6–12: Sc in each st around.

Rnd 13: [Sc in each of next 3 sts, sc dec in next 2 sts] around. *(24 sc)*

Rnd 14: [Sc in each of next 2 sts, sc dec in next 2 sts] around. *(18 sc)*

Rnd 15: [Sc dec in next 2 sts] around. *(9 sc)*

Rnd 16: [Sc dec in next 2 sts] 4 times, sl st in next st. Leaving long end, fasten off. *(5 sc)*

Weave long end through sts on last rnd, pull to close. Secure end.

Stuff Body, using eraser end of pencil to push stuffing down.

Using 12-inch end, sew Head to Body as shown in photo.

SNOUT
Rnd 1: With cream, ch 5, sc in 2nd ch from hook, sc in each of next 2 chs, 3 sc in last ch, working on opposite side of ch, sc in each of next 3 chs, 3 sc in last ch, **do not join**. *(12 sc)*

Rnd 2: [Sc in each of next 3 sts, 2 sc in each of next 3 sts] around. *(18 sc)*

Rnds 3 & 4: Sc in each st around. At end of last rnd, join in beg sc. Leaving 10-inch end, fasten off.

Stuff Snout.

Using 10-inch end, sew Snout to lower part of Head as shown in photo.

FINISHING
Using **satin stitch** *(see Fig. 1)*, with black, embroider eyes above Snout.

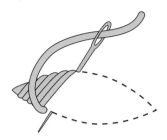

Fig. 1
Satin Stitch
(For Faces)

Using **straight stitch** *(see Fig. 2)*, with black, embroider 2 small sts on top of Snout for nostrils.

Fig. 2
Straight Stitch

Using straight stitch, with black, embroider mouth with 2 straight lines on Snout below nostrils as shown in photo.

EAR
MAKE 2.
Row 1: With fudge brown, ch 2, 6 sc in 2nd ch from hook, **do not join**, turn.

Row 2: Ch 1, sc in each of first 2 sts, 2 sc in each of next 2 sts, sc in each of last 2 sts. Leaving 8-inch end, fasten off.

Using 8-inch ends, sew Ears to rnds 8–12 on sides of Head as shown in photo.

ARM & LEG
MAKE 2 ARMS & 2 LEGS.
Rnd 1: Beg at top, with fudge brown, ch 11, sc in first ch to form ring, sc in each ch around, **do not join**. *(11 sc)*

Rnds 2–9: Sc in each st around. At end of last rnd, join in beg sc. Fasten off.

Rnd 10: Join cream with sc in first st, sc in next st, 2 sc in next st, sc in each of last 8 sts. *(12 sc)*

Rnd 11: Sc in each of first 3 sts, ch 3, 2 hdc in 2nd ch from hook, hdc in next ch *(thumb)*, sc in each of last 9 sts.

Rnd 12: Pushing thumb down to outside and working over it, sc in each st around.

Rnds 13–15: Sc in each st around.

Rnd 16: [Sc dec in next 2 sts] around, join in beg sc. Leaving long end, fasten off.

Weave long end through sts on last rnd, pull to close. Secure end.

Stuff Arms and Legs, leaving first 3 rnds unstuffed.

Flatten rnd 1 and sew closed.

Sew Arms to rnd 2 on Body and sew Legs to rnd 13 on Body as shown in photo.

TAIL
Row 1: With fudge brown, ch 18, hdc in 3rd ch from hook, hdc in each ch across, turn.

Row 2: Ch 1, working in **back lps** *(see Stitch Guide)* of hdc, fold piece in half lengthwise, working through both thicknesses, sl st row 1 to opposite side of beginning ch. Fasten off.

Sew 1 end of Tail to back of Body. ■

Itty Bitty
Elephant

SKILL LEVEL

INTERMEDIATE

FINISHED SIZE
3½ inches tall

MATERIALS
- Aunt Lydia's Classic Crochet size 10 crochet cotton (350 yds per ball):
  1 ball #332 hot pink
  25 yds #12 black
- Size 7/1.65mm steel crochet hook or size needed to obtain gauge
- Tapestry needle
- Fiberfill
- Stitch marker

GAUGE
9 sc = 1 inch

PATTERN NOTES
Work in continuous rounds, do not turn or join unless otherwise stated.

Mark first stitch of each round.

Join with slip stitch as indicated unless otherwise stated.

INSTRUCTIONS
ELEPHANT
HEAD
Rnd 1: Beg at top, with hot pink, ch 2, 6 sc in 2nd ch from hook, **do not join** (see Pattern Notes). (6 sc)

Rnd 2: 2 sc in each st around. (12 sc)

Rnd 3: [Sc in next st, 2 sc in next st] around. (18 sc)

Rnd 4: [Sc in each of next 2 sts, 2 sc in next st] around. (24 sc)

Rnd 5: [Sc in each of next 5 sts, 2 sc in next st] around. (28 sc)

Rnd 6: Sc in each st around.

Rnd 7: [Sc in each of next 13 sts, 2 sc in next st] around. (30 sc)

Rnds 8–13: Sc in each st around. At end of last rnd, stuff Head.

Rnd 14: [Sc in each of next 3 sts, **sc dec** (see Stitch Guide) in next 2 sts] around. (24 sc)

Rnd 15: [Sc in each of next 2 sts, sc dec in next 2 sts] around, **join** (see Pattern Notes) in beg sc. Leaving 12-inch end, fasten off. (18 sc)

Stuff Head completely.

BODY
Rnd 1: Beg in front, with hot pink, ch 2, 6 sc in 2nd ch from hook, **do not join**. (6 sc)

Rnd 2: 2 sc in each st around. (12 sc)

Rnd 3: [Sc in next st, 2 sc in next st] around. (18 sc)

Rnd 4: [Sc in each of next 2 sts, 2 sc in next st] around. (24 sc)

Rnd 5: [Sc in each of next 2 sts, 2 sc in next st] around. (32 sc)

Rnds 6–20: Sc in each st around. At end of last rnd, stuff Body. Continue to stuff as you work.

Rnd 21: [Sc in each of next 2 sts, sc dec in next 2 sts] around. (24 sc)

Rnd 22: [Sc in each of next 2 sts, sc dec in next 2 sts] around. (18 sc)

Rnd 23: [Sc in next st, sc dec in next 2 sts] around. (12 sc)

Finish stuffing Body.

Rnd 24: [Sc dec in next 2 sts] around, join in beg sc. Leaving long end, fasten off. (6 sc)

Weave long end through top of sts, pull to close. Secure end.

Using 12-inch end, sew Head to Body as shown in photo.

TRUNK
Rnd 1: Beg at tip, with hot pink, ch 2, 6 sc in 2nd ch from hook, **do not join**. (6 sc)

Rnd 2: [Sc in next st, 2 sc in next st] around. (9 sc)

Rnds 3 & 4: Sc in each st around.

Rnd 5: [Sc in each of next 2 sts, 2 sc in next st] around. (12 sc)

Rnds 6–8: Sc in each of first 5 sts, hdc in each of last 7 sts.

Rnd 9: [Sc in next st, 2 sc in next st] around. (18 sc)

Rnd 10: Sc in each st around.

Rnd 11: [Sc in each of next 2 sts, 2 sc in next st] around. *(24 sc)*

Rnd 12: Sc in each st around, join in beg sc. Leaving 10-inch end, fasten off.

Stuff Trunk, using eraser end of pencil to push stuffing down.

Using 10-inch end, sew Trunk to Head as shown in photo.

FINISHING

Using **satin stitch** *(see Fig. 1)*, with black, embroider eyes on Head above Trunk as shown in photo.

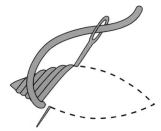

Fig. 1
Satin Stitch
(For Faces)

Using **straight stitch** *(see Fig. 2)*, with black, embroider mouth under Trunk as shown in photo.

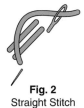

Fig. 2
Straight Stitch

EAR
MAKE 2.

Row 1: With hot pink, leaving 10-end, ch 10, sc in 2nd ch from hook and in each ch across, turn. *(9 sc)*

Rows 2 & 3: Ch 1, 2 sc in first st, sc in each st across with 2 sc in last st, turn. *(13 sc at end of last row)*

Rows 4–7: Ch 1, sc in each st across, turn.

Row 8: Ch 1, sk first st, sc dec in next 2 sts, sc in each of next 7 sts, sk next st, sc dec in next 2 sts. Fasten off.

Using 10-inch end, sew row 1 of Ears to rnds 5–14 at sides of Head as shown in photo.

LEG
MAKE 4.

Rnd 1: Beg at foot, with hot pink, ch 2, 7 sc in 2nd ch from hook, **do not join.** *(7 sc)*

Rnd 2: 2 sc in each st around. *(14 sc)*

Rnd 3: [Sc in next st, 2 sc in next st] around. *(21 sc)*

Rnd 4: Sc in each st around.

Rnd 5: [Sc dec in next 2 sts] 3 times, sc in each of last 15 sts. *(18 sc)*

Rnds 6–13: Sc in each st around. At end of last rnd, leaving 10-inch end, fasten off.

Stuff Legs.

Sew to bottom of Body as shown in photo.

TAIL

With hot pink, ch 7. Fasten off.

Cut 2 strands hot pink, each 4 inches long. Fold stands in half. Insert hook in last ch, pull fold through, pull ends of strands through fold. Pull to tighten. Trim strands to 1-inch in length.

Sew Tail to back of Body. ∎

Itty Bitty
Panda

SKILL LEVEL

INTERMEDIATE

FINISHED SIZE
3 inches tall

MATERIALS
- Aunt Lydia's Classic Crochet size 10 crochet cotton (white: 400 yds per ball; solids: 350 yds per ball; shades: 300 yds per ball):
  1 ball each #1 white and #12 black
  50 yds #453 shaded Christmas
- Size 7/1.65mm steel crochet hook or size needed to obtain gauge
- Tapestry needle
- Sewing needle
- Sewing thread:
  Black and white
- 5mm black beads: 2
- 2-inch square black felt
- Fiberfill
- Stitch marker

GAUGE
9 sc = 1 inch

PATTERN NOTES
Work in continuous rounds, do not turn or join unless otherwise stated.

Mark first stitch of each round.

Join with slip stitch as indicated unless otherwise stated.

INSTRUCTIONS
PANDA
HEAD
Rnd 1: Beg at snout, with white, ch 2, 4 sc in 2nd ch from hook, **do not join** (see Pattern Notes). (4 sc)

Rnds 2 & 3: [Sc in next st, 2 sc in next st] around. (9 sc at end of last rnd)

Rnd 4: [Sc in each of next 2 sts, 2 sc in next st] around. (12 sc)

Rnd 5: Sc in each of first 4 sts, 2 sc in each of next 4 sts, sc in each of last 4 sts. (16 sc)

Rnd 6: Sc in each of first 6 sts, 2 sc in each of next 4 sts, sc in each of last 6 sts. (20 sc)

Rnd 7: [Sc in each of next 4 sts, 2 sc in next st] around. (24 sc)

Rnd 8: [Sc in each of next 3 sts, 2 sc in next st] around. (30 sc)

Rnds 9–14: Sc in each st around. Stuff Head.

Rnd 15: [Sc in each of next 3 sts, **sc dec** (*see Stitch Guide*) in next 2 sts] around. (*24 sc*)

Rnd 16: [Sc in each of next 2 sts, sc dec in next 2 sts] around. (*18 sc*)

Rnd 17: [Sc in next st, sc dec in next 2 sts] around. Finish stuffing Head. (*12 sc*)

Rnd 18: [Sc dec in next 2 sts] around, **join** (*see Pattern Notes*) in beg sc. Leaving long end, fasten off.

Weave long end through sts of last rnd, pull to close. Secure end.

BODY

Rnd 1: With white, leaving 12-inch end, ch 18, sc in first ch to form ring, sc in each ch around, **do not join**. (*18 sc*)

Rnd 2: [Sc in each of next 5 sts, 2 sc in next st] around, join in beg sc. Fasten off. (*21 sc*)

Rnd 3: Join black with sc in first st, sc in each st around, **do not join**.

Rnd 4: [Sc in each of next 6 sts, 2 sc in next st] around. (*24 sc*)

Rnd 5: [Sc in each of next 3 sts, 2 sc in next st] around, join in beg sc. Fasten off. (*30 sc*)

Rnd 6: Join white with sc in first st, sc in each st around, **do not join**.

Rnds 7–12: Sc in each st around.

Rnd 13: [Sc in each of next 3 sts, sc dec in next 2 sts] around. (*24 sc*)

Rnd 14: [Sc in each of next 2 sts, sc dec in next 2 sts] around. (*18 sc*)

Rnd 15: [Sc dec in next 2 sts] around. (*9 sc*)

Rnd 16: [Sc dec in next 2 sts] 4 times, sl st in last st. Leaving long end, fasten off.

Weave long end through sts of last rnd, pull to close. Secure end.

Stuff Body, using eraser end of pencil to push stuffing down.

Using 12-inch end, sew Head to Body as shown in photo.

FINISHING

Using white sewing thread, sew beads to Head for eyes above snout as shown in photo.

Cut 2 ovals, each ¾-inch long, from black felt. Cut slit from center bottom up ¾ way to top. Fit felt around beads. Using black sewing thread, sew in place.

Using **satin stitch** (*see Fig. 1*), with black, embroider triangle on top of snout for nose as shown in photo.

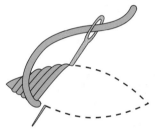

Fig. 1
Satin Stitch
(For Faces)

Using **straight stitch** (*see Fig. 2*), with black, make vertical line down from point of snout, then make V-shaped mouth with 2 straight stitches as shown in photo.

Fig. 2
Straight Stitch

EAR
MAKE 2.

Row 1: With black, ch 2, 6 sc in 2nd ch from hook, **do not join**, turn. (*6 sc*)

Row 2: Sc in first st, hdc in next st, 2 hdc in each of next 2 sts, hdc in next st, sc in last st. Leaving 8-inch end, fasten off.

Using 8-inch ends, sew Ears to top of Head as shown in photo.

LEG
MAKE 2.
Rnd 1: Beg at foot, with black, ch 2, 6 sc in 2nd ch from hook, **do not join**. *(6 sc)*

Rnd 2: 2 sc in first st, sc in next st, 2 hdc in each of next 2 sts, sc in next st, 2 sc in last st. *(10 sc)*

Rnd 3: 2 sc in first st, sc in each of next 2 sts, 2 sc in each of next 4 sts, sc in next st, 2 sc in next st, sc in last st. *(16 sc)*

Rnd 4: Sc in each st around.

Rnd 5: Sc in each of first 5 sts, [sc dec in next 2 sts] 3 times, sc in each of last 5 sts. *(13 sc)*

Rnd 6: Sc in each of first 5 sts, sc dec in next 2 sts, sc in each of last 6 sts. *(12 sc)*

Rnds 7 & 8: Sc in each st around.

Rnd 9: [Sc in each of next 2 sts, 2 sc in next st] around. *(16 sc)*

Rnd 10: [Sc in each of next 7 sts, 2 sc in next st] around, join in beg sc. Leaving 12-inch end, fasten off.

Stuff Legs.

Using 12-inch end, sew Legs to front bottom of Body as shown in photo so Panda is in sitting position.

ARM
MAKE 2.
Rnd 1: Beg at top, with black, ch 11, sc in first ch to form ring, sc in each ch around. *(11 sc)*

Rnds 2–6: Sc in each st around.

Rnd 7: Sc in each of first 4 sts, 2 sc in each of next 3 sts, sc in each of last 4 sts. *(14 sc)*

Rnds 8 & 9: Sc in each st around.

Rnd 10: [Sc in next st, sc dec in next 2 sts, sc in each of next 2 sts, sc dec in next 2 sts] around. *(10 sc)*

Rnd 11: [Sc dec in next 2 sts] around, join in beg sc. Leaving long end, fasten off.

Weave long end through sts on last rnd, pull to close. Secure end.

Stuff Arms, using eraser end of pencil to push stuffing down, leaving first 3 rnds unstuffed.

Flatten rnd 1 and sew closed.

Sew Arms to Body as shown in photo.

SCARF
Row 1: With shaded Christmas, ch 3, sc in 2nd ch from hook and in next ch, turn. *(2 sc)*

Rows 2–43: Ch 1, sc in each st across, turn. At end of last row, fasten off.

FRINGE
Cut 8 strands shaded Christmas, each 3 inches in length. Holding 2 strands tog, fold in half. Pull fold through st, pull ends through fold. Pull to tighten.

Attach 2 Fringe to each short end of Scarf. Trim. ■

Itty Bitty
Ballerina Bear

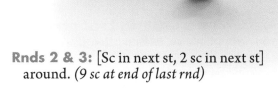

SKILL LEVEL

INTERMEDIATE

FINISHED SIZE
3 inches tall

MATERIALS
- Aunt Lydia's Classic Crochet size 10 crochet cotton (solids: 350 yds per ball; shades: 300 yds per ball):
  1 ball each #420 cream and
  #15 shaded pinks
  50 yds #0210 antique white and #12 black
- Size 7/1.65mm steel crochet hook or size needed to obtain gauge
- Tapestry needle
- Fiberfill
- Stitch marker

GAUGE
9 sc = 1 inch

PATTERN NOTES
Work in continuous rounds, do not turn or join unless otherwise stated.

Mark first stitch of each round.

Join with slip stitch as indicated unless otherwise stated.

Chain-3 at beginning of row or round counts as first double crochet unless otherwise stated.

INSTRUCTIONS
BALLERINA
HEAD
Rnd 1: Beg at snout, with antique white, ch 2, 4 sc in 2nd ch from hook, **do not join** *(see Pattern Notes)*. *(4 sc)*

Rnds 2 & 3: [Sc in next st, 2 sc in next st] around. *(9 sc at end of last rnd)*

Rnd 4: [Sc in each of next 2 sts, 2 sc in next st] around. *(12 sc)*

Rnd 5: Sc in each of first 4 sts, 2 sc in each of next 4 sts, sc in each of last 4 sts. Fasten off. *(16 sc)*

Rnd 6: Join cream with sc in first st, sc in each of next 5 sts, 2 sc in each of next 4 sts, sc in each of last 6 sts. *(20 sc)*

Rnd 7: [Sc in each of next 4 sts, 2 sc in next st] around. *(24 sc)*

Rnd 8: [Sc in each of next 3 sts, 2 sc in next st] around. *(30 sc)*

Rnds 9–14: Sc in each st around. Stuff Head.

Rnd 15: [Sc in each of next 3 sts, **sc dec** *(see Stitch Guide)* in next 2 sts] around. *(24 sc)*

Rnd 16: [Sc in each of next 2 sts, sc dec in next 2 sts] around. *(18 sc)*

Rnd 17: [Sc in next st, sc dec in next 2 sts] around. Finish stuffing Head. *(12 sc)*

Rnd 18: [Sc dec in next 2 sts] around, **join** (see Pattern Notes) in beg sc. Leaving long end, fasten off.

Weave long end through sts of last rnd, pull to close. Secure end.

BODY
Rnd 1: With cream, leaving 12-inch end, ch 18, sc in first ch to form ring, sc in each ch around, **do not join**. (18 sc)

Rnd 2: [Sc in each of next 5 sts, 2 sc in next st] around. (21 sc)

Rnd 3: Sc in each st around, **do not join**.

Rnd 4: [Sc in each of next 6 sts, 2 sc in next st] around. (24 sc)

Rnd 5: [Sc in each of next 3 sts, 2 sc in next st] around, join in beg sc. Fasten off. (30 sc)

Rnd 6: Working in **back lps** (see Stitch Guide), join shaded pinks with sc in first st, sc in each st around, **do not join**.

Rnds 7–12: Sc in each st around.

Rnd 13: [Sc in each of next 3 sts, sc dec in next 2 sts] around. (24 sc)

Rnd 14: [Sc in each of next 2 sts, sc dec in next 2 sts] around. (18 sc)

Rnd 15: [Sc dec in next 2 sts] around. (9 sc)

Rnd 16: [Sc dec in next 2 sts] 4 times, sl st in last st. Leaving long end, fasten off.

Weave long end through sts of last rnd, pull to close. Secure end.

Stuff Body, using eraser end of pencil to push stuffing down.

Using 12-inch end, sew Head to Body as shown in photo.

FINISHING
Using **satin stitch** (see Fig. 1), with black, embroider eyes to Head above snout and triangle on top of snout for nose as shown in photo.

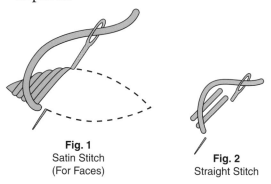

Fig. 1
Satin Stitch
(For Faces)

Fig. 2
Straight Stitch

Using **straight stitch** (see Fig. 2), with black, make vertical line down from point of snout, then make V-shaped mouth with 2 straight stitches as shown in photo.

EAR
MAKE 2.
Row 1: With antique white, ch 2, 6 sc in 2nd ch from hook, **do not join or turn**. Fasten off. (6 sc)

Row 2: Join cream with sc in first st, hdc in next st, 2 hdc in each of next 2 sts, hdc in next st, sc in last st. Leaving 10-inch end, fasten off.

Using 10-inch ends, sew Ears to rnds 10 and 11 on Head as shown in photo.

LEG
MAKE 2.
Rnd 1: Beg at foot, with shaded pinks, ch 2, 6 sc in 2nd ch from hook, **do not join**. (6 sc)

Rnd 2: 2 sc in first st, sc in next st, 2 hdc in each of next 2 sts, sc in next st, 2 sc in last st. (10 sc)

Rnd 3: 2 sc in first st, sc in each of next 2 sts, 2 sc in each of next 4 sts, sc in next st, 2 sc in next st, sc in last st. (16 sc)

Rnd 4: Sc in each st around, join in beg sc. Fasten off.

Rnd 5: Join cream with sc in first st, sc in each of next 4 sts, [sc dec in next 2 sts] 3 times, sc in each of last 5 sts. (13 sc)

Rnd 6: Sc in each of first 5 sts, sc dec in next 2 sts, sc in each of last 6 sts. *(12 sc)*

Rnds 7 & 8: Sc in each st around.

Rnd 9: [Sc in each of next 2 sts, 2 sc in next st] around. *(16 sc)*

Rnd 10: [Sc in each of next 7 sts, 2 sc in next st] around, join in beg sc. Leaving 12-inch end, fasten off.

Stuff Legs.

Using 12-inch end, sew Legs to front bottom of Body as shown in photo so Bear is in sitting position.

SHOE TIE
Cut 10-inch length of shaded pinks. Thread under 4 sts at front of toe, pulling out so ends are even. Cross over at front, take ends to back, cross over, bring back to front and tie in bow.

Rep on rem Leg.

ARM
MAKE 2.
Rnd 1: Beg at top, with cream, ch 11, sc in first ch to form ring, sc in each ch around. *(11 sc)*

Rnds 2–6: Sc in each st around.

Rnd 7: Sc in each of first 4 sts, 2 sc in each of next 3 sts, sc in each of last 4 sts. *(14 sc)*

Rnds 8 & 9: Sc in each st around.

Rnd 10: [Sc in next st, sc dec in next 2 sts, sc in each of next 2 sts, sc dec in next 2 sts] around. *(10 sc)*

Rnd 11: [Sc dec in next 2 sts] around, join in beg sc. Leaving long end, fasten off.

Weave long end through sts on last rnd, pull to close. Secure end.

Stuff Arms, using eraser end of pencil to push stuffing down, leaving first 3 rnds unstuffed.

Flatten rnd 1 and sew closed.

Sew Arms to Body as shown in photo.

TUTU
SKIRT
Rnd 1: Working in rem lps on rnd 5 of Body, join shaded pinks at center back, **ch 3** *(see Pattern Notes)*, 3 dc in same st, 4 dc in each st around, join in 3rd ch of beg ch-3. *(120 dc)*

Rnd 2: Ch 3, 2 dc in next st, [dc in next st, 2 dc in next st] around, join in 3rd ch of beg ch-3. *(180 dc)*

Rnd 3: Ch 1, sc in first st, sc in each st around, join in beg sc.

Rnd 4: Ch 1, sc in first st, [ch 2, sc in next st] around, ch 2, join in beg sc. Fasten off.

TOP
Row 1: Beg at waist, with shaded pinks, ch 9, sc in 2nd ch from hook and in each ch across, turn. *(8 sc)*

Row 2: Ch 2, sc dec in first 2 sts, sc in next st, sl st in each of next 2 sts, sc in next st, sc dec in last 2 sts, turn. *(6 sts)*

Row 3: Ch 2, **dc dec** *(see Stitch Guide)* in first 2 sts, ch 2, sl st in last st worked in, sl st in each of next 2 sts, ch 2, dc dec in next 2 sts, ch 2, sl st in last st worked in. Fasten off.

Sew row 1 of Top to front waist of Bottom.

STRAPS
Join shaded pinks in first dc dec on row 3 of Top, ch 35. Fasten off.

Rep in 2nd dc dec on same row of Top.

Tie Straps in bow at back of neck.

FLOWER
With shaded pinks, [ch 4, sl st in first ch] 5 times. Fasten off.

Gather up center and sew closed.

Sew Flower in front of right Ear as shown in photo. ∎

Itty Bitty
Baby Bear

SKILL LEVEL

INTERMEDIATE

FINISHED SIZE
3 inches tall

MATERIALS
- Aunt Lydia's Classic Crochet size 10 crochet cotton (white: 400 yds per ball; solids: 350 yds per ball; shades: 300 yds per ball):
  1 ball #420 cream and #465 pastels ombre
  100 yds each #0210 antique white and #1 white
  50 yds each #424 light peach and #12 black
- Size 7/1.65mm steel crochet hook or size needed to obtain gauge
- Tapestry needle
- Fiberfill
- Stitch marker

GAUGE
9 sc = 1 inch

PATTERN NOTES
Work in continuous rounds, do not turn or join unless otherwise stated.

Mark first stitch of each round.

Join with slip stitch as indicated unless otherwise stated.

Chain-3 at beginning of row or round counts as first double crochet unless otherwise stated.

INSTRUCTIONS
BABY BEAR
HEAD
Rnd 1: Beg at snout, with antique white, ch 2, 4 sc in 2nd ch from hook, **do not join** (see Pattern Notes). (4 sc)

Rnds 2 & 3: [Sc in next st, 2 sc in next st] around. (9 sc at end of last rnd)

Rnd 4: [Sc in each of next 2 sts, 2 sc in next st] around. (12 sc)

Rnd 5: Sc in each of first 4 sts, 2 sc in each of next 4 sts, sc in each of last 4 sts, **join** (see Pattern Notes) in beg sc. Fasten off. (16 sc)

Rnd 6: Join cream with sc in first st, sc in each of next 5 sts, 2 sc in each of next 4 sts, sc in each of last 6 sts, **do not join**. (20 sc)

Rnd 7: [Sc in each of next 4 sts, 2 sc in next st] around. (24 sc)

Rnd 8: [Sc in each of next 3 sts, 2 sc in next st] around. (30 sc)

Rnds 9–14: Sc in each st around. Stuff Head.

Rnd 15: [Sc in each of next 3 sts, **sc dec** (see Stitch Guide) in next 2 sts] around. (24 sc)

Rnd 16: [Sc in each of next 2 sts, sc dec in next 2 sts] around. (18 sc)

Rnd 17: [Sc in next st, sc dec in next 2 sts] around. Finish stuffing Head. *(12 sc)*

Rnd 18: [Sc dec in next 2 sts] around, join in beg sc. Leaving long end, fasten off.

Weave long end through sts of last rnd, pull to close. Secure end.

BODY

Rnd 1: With cream, leaving 12-inch end, ch 18, sc in first ch to form ring, sc in each ch around, **do not join**. *(18 sc)*

Rnd 2: [Sc in each of next 5 sts, 2 sc in next st] around. *(21 sc)*

Rnd 3: Sc in each st around.

Rnd 4: [Sc in each of next 6 sts, 2 sc in next st] around. *(24 sc)*

Rnd 5: [Sc in each of next 3 sts, 2 sc in next st] around. *(30 sc)*

Rnds 6–12: Sc in each st around.

Rnd 13: [Sc in each of next 3 sts, sc dec in next 2 sts] around. *(24 sc)*

Rnd 14: [Sc in each of next 2 sts, sc dec in next 2 sts] around. *(18 sc)*

Rnd 15: [Sc dec in next 2 sts] around. *(9 sc)*

Rnd 16: [Sc dec in next 2 sts] 4 times, sl st in last st. Leaving long end, fasten off.

Weave long end through sts of last rnd, pull to close. Secure end.

Stuff Body, using eraser end of pencil to push stuffing down.

Using 12-inch end, sew Head to Body as shown in photo.

FINISHING

Using **satin stitch** *(see Fig. 1)*, with black, embroider eyes on Head above snout and triangle on top of snout for nose as shown in photo.

Using **straight stitch** *(see Fig. 2)*, with black, make vertical line down from point of snout, then make V-shaped mouth with 2 straight stitches as shown in photo.

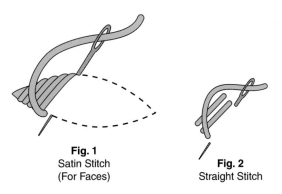

Fig. 1
Satin Stitch
(For Faces)

Fig. 2
Straight Stitch

EAR
MAKE 2.

Row 1: With antique white, ch 2, 6 sc in 2nd ch from hook, **do not join**, turn. Fasten off. *(6 sc)*

Row 2: Join cream with sc in first st, hdc in next st, 2 hdc in each of next 2 sts, hdc in next st, sc in last st. Leaving 8-inch end, fasten off.

Using 8-inch ends, sew Ears to rnds 10 and 11 of Head as shown in photo.

LEG
MAKE 2.

Rnd 1: Beg at foot, with antique white, ch 2, 6 sc in 2nd ch from hook, **do not join**. *(6 sc)*

Rnd 2: 2 sc in first st, sc in next st, 2 hdc in each of next 2 sts, sc in next st, 2 sc in last st. Fasten off. *(10 sc)*

Rnd 3: Join cream with sc in first st, sc in same st, sc in each of next 2 sts, 2 sc in each of next 4 sts, sc in next st, 2 sc in next st, sc in last st. *(16 sc)*

Rnd 4: Sc in each st around.

Rnd 5: Sc in each of first 5 sts, [sc dec in next 2 sts] 3 times, sc in each of last 5 sts. *(13 sc)*

Rnd 6: Sc in each of first 5 sts, sc dec in next 2 sts, sc in each of last 6 sts. *(12 sc)*

Rnds 7 & 8: Sc in each st around.

Rnd 9: [Sc in each of next 2 sts, 2 sc in next st] around. *(16 sc)*

Rnd 10: [Sc in each of next 7 sts, 2 sc in next st] around, join in beg sc. Leaving 12-inch end, fasten off.

Stuff Legs.

Using 12-inch end, sew Legs to front bottom of Body as shown in photo so Bear is in sitting position.

ARM
MAKE 2.
Rnd 1: Beg at top, with cream, ch 11, sc in first ch to form ring, sc in each ch around. *(11 sc)*

Rnds 2–6: Sc in each st around.

Rnd 7: Sc in each of first 4 sts, 2 sc in each of next 3 sts, sc in each of last 4 sts. *(14 sc)*

Rnds 8 & 9: Sc in each st around.

Rnd 10: [Sc in next st, sc dec in next 2 sts, sc in each of next 2 sts, sc dec in next 2 sts] around. *(10 sc)*

Rnd 11: [Sc dec in next 2 sts] around, join in beg sc. Leaving long end, fasten off.

Weave long end through sts on last rnd, pull to close. Secure end.

Stuff Arms, using eraser end of pencil to push stuffing down, leaving first 3 rnds unstuffed.

Flatten rnd 1 and sew closed.

Sew Arms to Body as shown in photo.

DIAPER
Row 1: Beg at waist back, with white, ch 19, sc in 2nd ch from hook and in each ch across, turn. *(18 sc)*

Rows 2–4: Ch 1, sc in each st across, turn.

Rows 5–7: Ch 1, sc dec in first 2 sts, sc in each st across with sc dec in last 2 sts, turn. *(12 sc at end of last row)*

Rows 8–10: Ch 1, sc in each st across, turn.

Rows 11–13: Rep rows 5–7. *(6 sc at end of last row)*

Rows 14–22: Ch 1, sc in each st across, turn.

Rows 23 & 24: Ch 1, 2 sc in first st, sc in each st across with 2 sc in last st, turn. *(10 sc at end of last row)*

Row 25: Ch 1, 2 sc in first st, sc in each st across with 2 sc in last st, turn. *(12 sc)*

Row 26: Ch 7, hdc in 3rd ch from hook, hdc in each of next 4 chs, sc in each of next 12 sts, ch 7, hdc in 3rd ch from hook, hdc in each of next 4 chs, sl st in end of last row. Fasten off.

Place Diaper on Bear, sew front tabs to row 1 at sides of back.

BOTTLE
Rnd 1: Beg at nipple, with light peach, ch 2, 4 sc in 2nd ch from hook, **do not join**. *(4 sc)*

Rnd 2: Sc in each st around.

Rnd 3: 2 sc in each st around, join in beg sc. Fasten off. *(8 sc)*

Rnd 4: Working in **back lps** *(see Stitch Guide)*, join white with sc in first st, sc in each st around.

Rnds 5–10: Sc in each st around. Stuff.

Rnd 11: Working in back lps, sk first st, sl st in next st, [sk next st, sl st in next st] around. Fasten off.

Sew end closed.

Sew Bottle to hand as shown in photo.

BIB
Row 1: Beg at neck, with white, ch 7, sc in 2nd ch from hook and in each ch across, turn. *(6 sc)*

Row 2: Ch 1, sc dec in first 2 sts, sc in each of next 2 sts, sc dec in last 2 sts, turn. *(4 sc)*

Row 3: Sc dec in first 2 sts, sc dec in last 2 sts. Fasten off. *(2 sc)*

EDGING

With pastels, ch 35 *(tie)*, working along edge of Bib in ends of rows, sc in end of first row, sc in each of next 2 rows, 3 sc in each of next 2 sts on row 3, sc in end of each of next 2 rows, sc in end of last row, ch 35 *(tie)*. Fasten off.

Place Bib around neck and tie in bow around neck.

BLANKET

Row 1: With pastels, ch 26, sc in 2nd ch from hook and in each ch across, turn. *(25 sc)*

Row 2: Ch 3 *(see Pattern Notes)*, 2 dc in same st, [sk next 3 sts, 5 dc in next st] 5 times, sk next 3 sts, 3 dc in last st, turn.

Rows 3–11: Ch 3, 2 dc in same st, 5 dc in center dc of each dc group across, ending with 3 dc in last st, turn. At end of last row, **do not turn**.

Rnd 4: Working around outer edge and in ends of rows, ch 1, [sc in end of next row, ch 2] across, working in starting ch on opposite side of row 1, sc in first ch, [ch 2, sk next 2 chs, sc in next ch] across, working in ends of rows, [ch 2, sc in end of next row] across, ch 2, sc in first st, ch 2, sk next st, sc in next st, [ch 2, sk next 2 sts, sc in center st of dc group, ch 2, sk next 2 sts, sc in sp between dc groups] 5 times, ch 2, sk next st, sl st in last st. Fasten off. ■

Itty Bitty Chef Bear

SKILL LEVEL

INTERMEDIATE

FINISHED SIZE

3½ inches tall

MATERIALS

- Aunt Lydia's Classic Crochet size 10 crochet cotton (white: 400 yds per ball; solids: 350 yds per ball):
    1 ball each #21 linen and #1 white
    100 yds each #420 cream and #226 natural
    50 yds each #494 victory red, #1056 chambray and #12 black
- Size 7/1.65mm steel crochet hook or size needed to obtain gauge
- Tapestry needle
- Fiberfill
- Stitch marker

GAUGE
9 sc = 1 inch

PATTERN NOTES
Work in continuous rounds, do not turn or join unless otherwise stated.

Mark first stitch of each round.

Join with slip stitch as indicated unless otherwise stated.

Chain-3 at beginning of row or round counts as first double crochet unless otherwise stated.

INSTRUCTIONS
CHEF
HEAD
Rnd 1: Beg at snout, with cream, ch 2, 4 sc in 2nd ch from hook, **do not join** (see Pattern Notes). (4 sc)

Rnds 2 & 3: [Sc in next st, 2 sc in next st] around. (9 sc at end of last rnd)

Rnd 4: [Sc in each of next 2 sts, 2 sc in next st] around. (12 sc)

Rnd 5: Sc in each of first 4 sts, 2 sc in each of next 4 sts, sc in each of last 4 sts, **join** (see Pattern Notes) in beg sc. Fasten off. (16 sc)

Rnd 6: Join linen with sc in first st, sc in each of next 5 sts, 2 sc in each of next 4 sts, sc in each of last 6 sts. (20 sc)

Rnd 7: [Sc in each of next 4 sts, 2 sc in next st] around. (24 sc)

Rnd 8: [Sc in each of next 3 sts, 2 sc in next st] around. (30 sc)

Rnds 9–14: Sc in each st around. Stuff Head.

Rnd 15: [Sc in each of next 3 sts, **sc dec** (see Stitch Guide) in next 2 sts] around. (24 sc)

Rnd 16: [Sc in each of next 2 sts, sc dec in next 2 sts] around. (18 sc)

Rnd 17: [Sc in next st, sc dec in next 2 sts] around. Finish stuffing Head. (12 sc)

Rnd 18: [Sc dec in next 2 sts] around, join in beg sc. Leaving long end, fasten off.

Weave long end through sts of last rnd, pull to close. Secure end.

BODY
Rnd 1: With linen, leaving 12-inch end, ch 18, sc in first ch to form ring, sc in each ch around, **do not join**. (18 sc)

Rnd 2: [Sc in each of next 5 sts, 2 sc in next st] around. (21 sc)

Rnd 3: Sc in each st around.

Rnd 4: [Sc in each of next 6 sts, 2 sc in next st] around. (24 sc)

Rnd 5: [Sc in each of next 3 sts, 2 sc in next st] around. (30 sc)

Rnds 6–12: Sc in each st around.

Rnd 13: [Sc in each of next 3 sts, sc dec in next 2 sts] around. (24 sc)

Rnd 14: [Sc in each of next 2 sts, sc dec in next 2 sts] around. (18 sc)

Rnd 15: [Sc dec in next 2 sts] around. (9 sc)

Rnd 16: [Sc dec in next 2 sts] 4 times, sl st in last st. Leaving long end, fasten off.

Weave long end through sts of last rnd, pull to close. Secure end.

Stuff Body, using eraser end of pencil to push stuffing down.

Using 12-inch end, sew Head to Body as shown in photo.

FINISHING
Using **satin stitch** (see Fig. 1), with black, embroider eyes above snout and triangle on top of snout for nose as shown in photo.

Using **straight stitch** (*see Fig. 2*), with black crochet cotton, make vertical line down from point of snout, then make V-shaped mouth with 2 straight stitches as shown in photo.

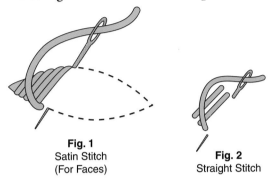

Fig. 1
Satin Stitch
(For Faces)

Fig. 2
Straight Stitch

LEG
MAKE 2

Rnd 1: Beg at foot, with cream, ch 2, 6 sc in 2nd ch from hook, **do not join**. *(6 sc)*

Rnd 2: 2 sc in first st, sc in next st, 2 hdc in each of next 2 sts, sc in next st, 2 sc in last st. Fasten off. *(10 sc)*

Rnd 3: Join linen with sc in first st, sc in same st, sc in each of next 2 sts, 2 sc in each of next 4 sts, sc in next st, 2 sc in next st, sc in last st. *(16 sc)*

Rnd 4: Sc in each st around.

Rnd 5: Sc in each of first 5 sts, [sc dec in next 2 sts] 3 times, sc in each of last 5 sts. *(13 sc)*

Rnd 6: Sc in each of first 5 sts, sc dec in next 2 sts, sc in each of last 6 sts. *(12 sc)*

Rnds 7 & 8: Sc in each st around.

Rnd 9: [Sc in each of next 2 sts, 2 sc in next st] around. *(16 sc)*

Rnd 10: [Sc in each of next 7 sts, 2 sc in next st] around, join in beg sc. Leaving 12-inch end, fasten off.

Stuff Legs.

Using 12-inch end, sew Legs to front bottom of Body as shown in photo so Bear is in sitting position.

ARM
MAKE 2.

Rnd 1: Beg at top, with linen, ch 11, sc in first ch to form ring, sc in each ch around. *(11 sc)*

Rnds 2–6: Sc in each st around.

Rnd 7: Sc in each of first 4 sts, 2 sc in each of next 3 sts, sc in each of last 4 sts. *(14 sc)*

Rnds 8 & 9: Sc in each st around.

Rnd 10: [Sc in next st, sc dec in next 2 sts, sc in each of next 2 sts, sc dec in next 2 sts] around. *(10 sc)*

Rnd 11: [Sc dec in next 2 sts] around, join in beg sc. Leaving long end, fasten off.

Weave long end through sts on last rnd, pull to close. Secure end.

Stuff Arms, using eraser end of pencil to push stuffing down, leaving first 3 rnds unstuffed.

Flatten rnd 1 and sew closed.

Sew Arms to Body as shown in photo.

EAR
MAKE 2.

Row 1: With cream, ch 2, 6 sc in 2nd ch from hook, **do not join**, turn. Fasten off. *(6 sc)*

Row 2: Join linen with sc in first st, hdc in next st, 2 hdc in each of next 2 sts, hdc in next st, sc in last st. Leaving 8-inch end, fasten off.

HAT

Rnd 1: With white, ch 24, sc in first ch to form ring, sc in each ch around. *(24 sc)*

Rnds 2 & 3: Sc in each st around.

Rnd 4: Sl st in next st, **ch 3** (*see Pattern Notes*), 2 dc in same st, 3 dc in each st around, join in 3rd ch of beg ch-3. *(72 dc)*

Rnds 5 & 6: Ch 3, dc in each st around, join in 3rd ch of beg ch-3.

Rnd 7: Ch 3, **dc dec** (*see Stitch Guide*) in next 2 sts, [dc in next st, dc dec in next 2 sts] around, join in 3rd ch of beg ch-3. *(48 dc)*

Rnds 8 & 9: Ch 3, dc dec in same st and in next st, [dc dec in next 2 sts] around. *(12 dc at end of last rnd)*

Rnd 10: Ch 1, sc dec in first 2 sts, [sc dec in next 2 sts] around, join in beg sc. Fasten off.

Sew Hat to top of Head.

Sew Ears to Head in front of Hat as shown in photo.

APRON
Row 1: Beg at bib, with white, ch 6, sc in 2nd ch from hook and in each ch across, turn. *(5 sc)*

Rows 2 & 3: 2 sc in first st, sc in each st across to last st, 2 sc in last st, turn. *(9 sc at end of last row)*

Rows 4–8: Ch 1, sc in each st, across, turn.

Row 9: Ch 1, sc in each st across. Fasten off.

TOP TIES
Join white at top corner of bib, ch 26. Fasten off.

Rep on rem top corner of bib.

SIDE TIES
Join white at side of Apron between rows 4 and 5, ch 26. Fasten off.

Rep on opposite side of Apron.

Place Apron on Bear, tie Top Ties in bow at back of neck.

Tie Side Ties in bow at back of waist.

PIE
FILLING
Rnd 1: With victory red, ch 2, 8 sc in 2nd ch from hook, **do not join**. *(8 sc)*

Rnd 2: 2 sc in each st around. Fasten off. *(16 sc)*

CRUST
Rnd 1: With natural, ch 2, 6 sc in 2nd ch from hook, **do not join**. *(6 sc)*

Rnd 2: 2 sc in each st around. *(12 sc)*

Rnd 3: [Sc in each of next 2 sts, 2 sc in next st] around, join in beg sc. *(16 sc)*

Rnd 4: Working in **back lps** (*see Stitch Guide*), ch 1, sc in each st around, join in beg sc, **turn**.

Rnd 5: Place Filling inside Crust, working through both thicknesses, in back lps of Filling and both lps of Crust, [sl st in next st, ch 2] around, join in beg sl st. Fasten off.

Tack Pie to Arm as shown in photo.

SPOON
With chambray, ch 7, sl st in 2nd ch from hook, sl st in each of next 4 chs, (sl st, ch 2, hdc, dc) in last ch, working on opposite side of ch, (dc, hdc, ch 2, sl st) in first ch, sl st in each of next 5 chs. Fasten off.

Tack Spoon to other Arm as shown in photo. ∎

Itty Bitty Uncle Sam

SKILL LEVEL

INTERMEDIATE

FINISHED SIZE
3½ inches tall

MATERIALS
- Aunt Lydia's Classic Crochet size 10 crochet cotton (white: 400 yds per ball; solids: 350 yds per ball):
  1 ball each #1 white, #0310 copper mist, #487 dark royal and #494 victory red
  50 yds each #226 natural and #12 black
- Size 7/1.65mm steel crochet hook or size needed to obtain gauge
- Tapestry needle
- Fiberfill
- Stitch marker

GAUGE
9 sc = 1 inch

PATTERN NOTES
Work in continuous rounds, do not turn or join unless otherwise stated.

Mark first stitch of each round.

Join with slip stitch as indicated unless otherwise stated.

Chain-2 at beginning of row or round counts as first half double crochet unless otherwise stated.

INSTRUCTIONS
UNCLE SAM
HEAD
Rnd 1: Beg at snout, with natural, ch 2, 4 sc in 2nd ch from hook, **do not join** *(see Pattern Notes). (4 sc)*

Rnds 2 & 3: [Sc in next st, 2 sc in next st] around. *(9 sc at end of last rnd)*

Rnd 4: [Sc in each of next 2 sts, 2 sc in next st] around. *(12 sc)*

Rnd 5: Sc in each of first 4 sts, 2 sc in each of next 4 sts, sc in each of last 4 sts, **join** *(see Pattern Notes)* in beg sc. Fasten off. *(16 sc)*

Rnd 6: Join copper mist with sc in first st, sc in each of next 5 sts, 2 sc in each of next 4 sts, sc in each of last 6 sts. *(20 sc)*

Rnd 7: [Sc in each of next 4 sts, 2 sc in next st] around. *(24 sc)*

Rnd 8: [Sc in each of next 3 sts, 2 sc in next st] around. *(30 sc)*

Rnds 9–14: Sc in each st around. Stuff Head.

Rnd 15: [Sc in each of next 3 sts, **sc dec** *(see Stitch Guide)* in next 2 sts] around. *(24 sc)*

Rnd 16: [Sc in each of next 2 sts, sc dec in next 2 sts] around. *(18 sc)*

Rnd 17: [Sc in next st, sc dec in next 2 sts] around. Finish stuffing Head. *(12 sc)*

Rnd 18: [Sc dec in next 2 sts] around, join in beg sc. Leaving long end, fasten off.

Weave long end through sts of last rnd, pull to close. Secure end.

BODY

Rnd 1: With dark royal, leaving 12-inch end, ch 18, sc in first ch to form ring, sc in each ch around, **do not join.** *(18 sc)*

Rnd 2: [Sc in each of next 5 sts, 2 sc in next st] around. *(21 sc)*

Rnd 3: Sc in each st around.

Rnd 4: [Sc in each of next 6 sts, 2 sc in next st] around. *(24 sc)*

Rnd 5: [Sc in each of next 3 sts, 2 sc in next st] around. *(30 sc)*

Rnd 6: Sc in each st around, join in beg sc. Fasten off.

Rnd 7: Join white with sc in first st, sc in each st around.

Rnd 8: Sc in each st around, **changing color** *(see Stitch Guide)* to victory red in last st.

Rnds 9 & 10: Sc in each st around. At end of last rnd, change color to white in last st.

Rnds 11 & 12: Sc in each st around. At end of last rnd, change color to victory red in last st.

Rnd 13: [Sc in each of next 3 sts, sc dec in next 2 sts] around. *(24 sc)*

Rnd 14: [Sc in each of next 3 sts, sc dec in next 2 sts] around, changing to white in last st. Fasten off victory red. *(18 sc)*

Rnd 15: [Sc dec in next 2 sts] around. *(9 sc)*

Rnd 16: [Sc dec in next 2 sts] 4 times, sl st in last st. Leaving long end, fasten off.

Weave long end through sts of last rnd, pull to close. Secure end.

Stuff Body, using eraser end of pencil to push stuffing down.

Using 12-inch end, sew Head to Body as shown in photo.

FINISHING

Using **satin stitch** *(see Fig. 1)*, with black, embroider eyes above snout on Head and a triangle on top of snout for nose as shown in photo.

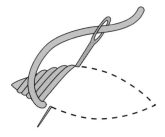

Fig. 1
Satin Stitch
(For Faces)

Using **straight stitch** *(see Fig. 2)*, with black, make vertical line down from point of snout, then make V-shaped mouth with 2 straight stitches as shown in photo.

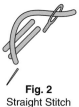

Fig. 2
Straight Stitch

LEG
MAKE 2.

Rnd 1: Beg at foot, with copper mist, ch 2, 6 sc in 2nd ch from hook, **do not join**. *(6 sc)*

Rnd 2: 2 sc in first st, sc in next st, 2 hdc in each of next 2 sts, sc in next st, 2 sc in last st. *(10 sts)*

Rnd 3: 2 sc in next st, sc in each of next 2 sts, 2 sc in each of next 4 sts, sc in next st, 2 sc in next st, sc in last st, join in beg sc. *(16 sc)*

Rnd 4: Working in **back lps** *(see Stitch Guide)*, ch 1, sc in each st around.

Rnd 5: Sc in each of first 5 sts, [sc dec in next 2 sts] 3 times, sc in each of last 5 sts. *(13 sc)*

Rnd 6: Sc in each of first 5 sts, sc dec in next 2 sts, sc in each of last 6 sts, join in beg sc. Fasten off.

Rnd 7: Join white with sc in first st, sc in each st around, **do not join**.

Rnd 8: Sc in each st around, join in beg sc. Fasten off.

Rnd 9: Join victory red with sc in first st, sc in next st, 2 sc in next st, [sc in each of next 2 sts, 2 sc in next st] around. *(16 sc)*

Rnd 10: [Sc in each of next 7 sts, 2 sc in next st] around, join in beg sc. Leaving 12-inch length, fasten off.

Stuff Legs, using eraser end of pencil to push stuffing down.

Sew Legs to bottom front on Body as shown in photo so Bear is in sitting position.

ARM
MAKE 2.

Rnd 1: Beg at top with dark royal, leaving 12-inch end, ch 11, sc in first ch to form ring, sc in each ch around. *(11 sc)*

Rnds 2–5: Sc in each st around. At end of last rnd, join in beg sc. Fasten off.

Rnd 6: Join white with sc in first st, sc in each st around, join in beg sc. Fasten off.

Rnd 7: Working in back lps, join copper mist with sc in first st, sc in each of next 3 sts, 2 sc in each of next 3 sts, sc in each of last 4 sts. *(14 sc)*

Rnds 8 & 9: Sc in each st around.

Rnd 10: [Sc in next st, sc dec in next 2 sts, sc in each of next 2 sts, sc dec in next 2 sts] around. *(10 sc)*

Rnd 11: [Sc dec in next 2 sts] around. Join in beg sc. Leaving long end, fasten off.

Weave long end through sts on last rnd, pull to close. Secure end.

Stuff Arms, using eraser end of pencil to push stuffing down, leaving first 3 rnds unstuffed.

Flatten rnd 1 and sew closed.

Sew Arms to side of Body as shown in photo.

CUFF STRIPE

Using straight stitch, with victory red, embroider vertical stitches between white sc on rnd 6 of Arm.

Rep on rem Arm.

COLLAR

With white, ch 23, hdc in 3rd ch from hook and in each ch across. Fasten off.

Sew Collar around neck, beg at center front.

BOW TIE

Row 1: With victory red, ch 5, sc in 2nd ch from hook and in each ch across, turn. *(4 sc)*

Row 2: Ch 1, sc dec in first 2 sts, sc dec in last 2 sts. *(2 sc)*

Row 3: Ch 1, sc dec in 2 sts. *(1 sc)*

Row 4: Ch 1, 2 sc in st, turn. *(2 sc)*

Row 5: 2 sc in each of next 2 sts, turn. *(4 sc)*

Row 6: Ch 1, sc in each st across. Fasten off.

Sew Bow Tie to top center front of Body as shown in photo.

SUSPENDER
MAKE 2.
Row 1: With white, ch 20. Fasten off.

Row 2: Join red with sc in first ch, sc in each ch across. Fasten off.

Sew 1 end of 1 Suspender to front waist above 1 Leg with red section on inside as shown in photo, sew other end to back waist.

Rep with rem Suspender on other side.

HAT
SIDE
Row 1: With victory red, ch 9, sc in 2nd ch from hook and in each ch across, turn. (8 sc)

Row 2: Ch 1, sc in each st across, changing color to white in last st, turn.

Row 3: Ch 1, sc in each st across, turn.

Row 4: Ch 1, sc in each st across, changing to victory red in last st, turn.

Row 5: Ch 1, sc in each st across, turn.

Row 6: Ch 1, sc in each st across, changing to white in last st, turn.

Rows 7–22: [Rep rows 3–6 consecutively] 4 times. At end of last row, fasten off victory red.

Row 23: With white, ch 1, sc in each st across, turn.

Row 24: Ch 1, sc in each st across. Leaving 10-inch end, fasten off.

Sew row 1 to row 24, forming tube.

BRIM
Rnd 1: Working in ends of rows on 1 edge of Side, join white with sc in end of first row, sc in same row, 2 sc in end of each row around, join in beg sc. (48 sc)

Rnd 2: Ch 2 (see Pattern Notes), hdc in each st around, join in 2nd ch of beg ch-2. Leaving 12-inch end, fasten off.

TOP
Rnd 1: With white, ch 2, 6 sc in 2nd ch from hook, **do not join**. (6 sc)

Rnd 2: 2 sc in each st around. (12 sc)

Rnd 3: [Sc in next st, 2 sc in next st] around. (18 sc)

Rnd 4: [Sc in each of next 2 sts, 2 sc in next st] around, join in beg sc. Leaving 12-inch end, fasten off.

Sew Top to other end of Side for top of Hat.

HAT BAND
Row 1: With dark royal, ch 33, sc in 2nd ch from hook and in each ch across, turn. (32 sc)

Row 2: Ch 1, sc in each st across. Leaving 12-inch end, fasten off.

Sew ends of rows tog, forming ring.

Place around Hat above Brim.

STARS
Using straight stitch, with white, embroider Stars around Hat Band by making an X with + on top of X.

Stuff Hat and sew to top of Head as shown in photo.

EAR
MAKE 2.
With copper mist, ch 3, (sc, hdc, dc) in 2nd ch from hook, (dc, hdc, sc) in last ch. Fasten off.

Sew Ears to rnd 1 on Brim of Hat. ■

Itty Bitty
Santa Bear

SKILL LEVEL

INTERMEDIATE

FINISHED SIZE
3 inches tall

MATERIALS
- Aunt Lydia's Classic Crochet size 10 crochet cotton (white: 400 yds per ball; solids: 350 yds per ball):
  1 ball each #21 linen and #494 victory red
  100 yds each #1 white, #420 cream, #12 black and #422 golden yellow
- Size 7/1.65mm steel crochet hook or size needed to obtain gauge
- Tapestry needle
- Fiberfill
- Stitch marker

GAUGE
9 sc = 1 inch

PATTERN NOTES
Work in continuous rounds, do not turn or join unless otherwise stated.

Mark first stitch of each round.

Join with slip stitch as indicated unless otherwise stated.

SPECIAL STITCH
Cluster (cl): Holding back last lp of each st on hook, 3 dc in place indicated, yo, pull though all lps on hook.

INSTRUCTIONS
SANTA
HEAD
Rnd 1: Beg at snout, with cream, ch 2, 4 sc in 2nd ch from hook, **do not join** (see Pattern Notes). (4 sc)

Rnds 2 & 3: [Sc in next st, 2 sc in next st] around. (9 sc at end of last rnd)

Rnd 4: [Sc in each of next 2 sts, 2 sc in next st] around. (12 sc)

Rnd 5: Sc in each of first 4 sts, 2 sc in each of next 4 sts, sc in each of last 4 sts, **join** (see Pattern Notes) in beg sc. Fasten off. (16 sc)

Rnd 6: Join linen with sc in first st, sc in each of next 5 sts, 2 sc in each of next 4 sts, sc in each of last 6 sts. (20 sc)

Rnd 7: [Sc in each of next 4 sts, 2 sc in next st] around. (24 sc)

Rnd 8: [Sc in each of next 3 sts, 2 sc in next st] around. (30 sc)

Rnds 9–14: Sc in each st around. Stuff Head.

Rnd 15: [Sc in each of next 3 sts, **sc dec** (see Stitch Guide) in next 2 sts] around. (24 sc)

Rnd 16: [Sc in each of next 2 sts, sc dec in next 2 sts] around. (18 sc)

Rnd 17: [Sc in next st, sc dec in next 2 sts] around. Finish stuffing Head. *(12 sc)*

Rnd 18: [Sc dec in next 2 sts] around, join in beg sc. Leaving long end, fasten off.

Weave long end through sts of last rnd, pull to close. Secure end.

BODY

Rnd 1: With victory red, leaving 12-inch end, ch 18, sc in first ch to form ring, sc in each ch around, **do not join.** *(18 sc)*

Rnd 2: [Sc in each of next 5 sts, 2 sc in next st] around, join in beg sc. *(21 sc)*

Rnd 3: Sc in each st around.

Rnd 4: [Sc in each of next 6 sts, 2 sc in next st] around. *(24 sc)*

Rnd 5: [Sc in each of next 3 sts, 2 sc in next st] around. *(30 sc)*

Rnd 6: Sc in each st around.

Rnd 7: Working this rnd in **back lps** *(see Stitch Guide)*, sc in each st around.

Rnds 8–12: Sc in each st around.

Rnd 13: [Sc in each of next 3 sts, sc dec in next 2 sts] around. *(24 sc)*

Rnd 14: [Sc in each of next 2 sts, sc dec in next 2 sts] around. *(18 sc)*

Rnd 15: [Sc dec in next 2 sts] around. *(9 sc)*

Rnd 16: [Sc dec in next 2 sts] 4 times, sl st in last st. Leaving long end, fasten off.

Weave long end through sts of last rnd, pull to close. Secure end.

Stuff Body, using eraser end of pencil to push stuffing down.

Using 12-inch end, sew Head to Body as shown in photo.

FINISHING

Using **satin stitch** *(see Fig. 1)*, with black, embroider eyes above snout as shown in photo and a triangle on top of snout for nose as shown in photo.

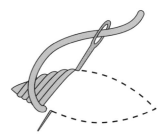

Fig. 1
Satin Stitch
(For Faces)

Using **straight stitch** *(see Fig. 2)*, with black, make vertical line down from point of snout, then make V-shaped mouth with 2 straight stitches as shown in photo.

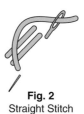

Fig. 2
Straight Stitch

COAT BOTTOM

Row 1: Beg at front, working in rem lps of rnd 6 on Body, with Head facing, join in first lp, ch 1, hdc in same st, hdc in each of next 3 sts, 2 hdc in next st, [hdc in each of next 4 sts, 2 hdc in next st] across, turn. *(36 hdc)*

Row 2: Ch 1, sc in each st across. Fasten off.

COAT TRIM

With victory red, ch 6. Fasten off. Place aside.

With Head facing you, join white with sc in end of row 1 of Coat Bottom on your left, sc in end of next row, working across Coat Bottom, 2 sc in first st, sc in each st across with 2 sc in last st, sc in end of next 2 rows, sc in each of ch-6 that was placed aside. Fasten off.

Sew chain to front of Coat as shown in photo.

BELT

With black, ch 34, sl st in 2nd ch from hook and in each ch across. Leaving 12-inch end, fasten off.

Place Belt around waist and sew in place.

Using straight stitch, with golden yellow, embroider square around center front of Belt as shown in photo.

LEG
MAKE 2.

Rnd 1: Beg at foot, with black, ch 2, 6 sc in 2nd ch from hook, **do not join**. (6 sc)

Rnd 2: 2 sc in first st, sc in next st, 2 hdc in each of next 2 sts, sc in next st, 2 sc in last st. (10 sc)

Rnd 3: 2 sc in first st, sc in each of next 2 sts, 2 sc in each of next 4 sts, sc in next st, 2 sc in next st, sc in last st. (16 sc)

Rnd 4: Sc in each st around.

Rnd 5: Sc in each of first 5 sts, [sc dec in next 2 sts] 3 times, sc in each of last 5 sts. (13 sc)

Rnd 6: Sc in each of first 5 sts, sc dec in next 2 sts, sc in each of last 6 sts, join in beg sc. Fasten off. (12 sc)

Rnd 7: Join victory red with sc in first st, sc in each st around.

Rnd 8: Sc in each st around.

Rnd 9: [Sc in each of next 2 sts, 2 sc in next st] around. (16 sc)

Rnd 10: [Sc in each of next 7 sts, 2 sc in next st] around, join in beg sc. Leaving 12-inch end, fasten off.

Stuff Legs.

Using 12-inch ends, sew Legs to front bottom of Body as shown in photo so Bear is in sitting position.

ARM
MAKE 2.

Rnd 1: Beg at top, with victory red, ch 11, sc in first ch to form ring, sc in each ch around. (11 sc)

Rnds 2–6: Sc in each st around. At end of last rnd, join in beg sc. Fasten off.

Rnd 7: Join linen with sc in first st, sc in each of next 3 sts, 2 sc in each of next 3 sts, sc in each of last 4 sts. (14 sc)

Rnds 8 & 9: Sc in each st around.

Rnd 10: [Sc in next st, sc dec in next 2 sts, sc in each of next 2 sts, sc dec in next 2 sts] around. (10 sc)

Rnd 11: [Sc dec in next 2 sts] around, join in beg sc. Leaving long end, fasten off.

Weave long end through sts on last rnd, pull to close. Secure end.

Stuff Arms, using eraser end of pencil to push stuffing down, leaving first 3 rnds unstuffed.

Flatten rnd 1 and sew closed.

Sew Arms to Body as shown in photo.

SLEEVE TRIM
MAKE 2.

With white, ch 14. Fasten off.

Sew 1 Sleeve Trim around each Arm on rnd 6.

COLLAR

With white, ch 21, sc in 2nd ch from hook and in each ch across. Fasten off.

Sew Collar around neck, beg at center front.

HAT

Rnd 1: Beg at brim, with white, ch 30, sc in first ch to form ring, sc in each ch around, **do not join**. (30 sc)

Rnd 2: Sc in each ch around, join in beg sc, **turn**.

Rnd 3: Working in back lps, ch 1, hdc in first st, hdc in each of next 3 sts, 2 hdc in next st, [hdc in each of next 4 sts, 2 hdc in next st] around, join in beg hdc. Fasten off.

Rnd 4: Working in starting ch on opposite side of rnd 1, join victory red with sc in first ch, sc in each of next 7 chs, ch 5, sk next 5 chs *(ear opening)*, sc in each of next 5 chs, ch 5, sk next 5 chs *(ear opening)*, sc in each of last 7 sts, **do not join.**

Rnd 5: Sc in each of next 8 sts, sc in each of next 5 chs, sc in each of next 5 sts, sc in each of next 5 chs, sc in each of last 7 chs. *(30 sc)*

Rnds 6–8: Sc in each st around.

Rnd 9: [Sc in each of next 13 sts, sc dec in next 2 sts] around. *(28 sc)*

Rnd 10: [Sc in each of next 5 sts, sc dec in next 2 sts] around. *(24 sc)*

Rnd 11: [Sc in each of next 4 sts, sc dec in next 2 sts] around. *(20 sc)*

Rnd 12: [Sc in each of next 3 sts, sc dec in next 2 sts] around. *(16 sc)*

Rnd 13: [Sc in each of next 6 sts, sc dec in next 2 sts] around. *(14 sc)*

Rnd 14: [Sc in each of next 5 sts, sc dec in next 2 sts] around. *(12 sc)*

Rnd 15: Sc in each st around.

Rnd 16: [Sc in each of next 4 sts, sc dec in next 2 sts] around. *(10 sc)*

Rnds 17–19: Sc in each st around.

Rnd 20: [Sc in each of next 3 sts, sc dec in next 2 sts] around. *(8 sc)*

Rnd 21: [Sc in each of next 2 sts, sc dec in next 2 sts] around. *(6 sc)*

Rnd 22: [Sc in next st, sc dec in next 2 sts] around, join in beg sc. Fasten off.

Bend tip of Hat to 1 side and tack in place.

POMPOM
With white, ch 3, **cl** *(see Special Stitch)* in 3rd ch from hook, ch 1, sl st in same ch. Fasten off.

Sew Pompom to tip of Hat.

EAR
MAKE 2.
Rnd 1: With cream, ch 2, 6 sc in 2nd ch from hook, **do not join.** Fasten off. *(6 sc)*

Rnd 2: Join linen with sc in first st, hdc in next st, 2 hdc in each of next 2 sts, hdc in next st, sc in last st. Leaving 10-inch end, fasten off.

Place Hat on Head, marking ear openings with pin.

Sew Ears to rnds 10 and 11 on Head.

Sew Hat to Head, pulling Ears through ear openings on Hat. ■

Stitch Guide

For more complete information, visit **FreePatterns.com**

ABBREVIATIONS

beg	begin/begins/beginning
bpdc	back post double crochet
bpsc	back post single crochet
bptr	back post treble crochet
CC	contrasting color
ch(s)	chain(s)
ch-	refers to chain or space previously made (e.g., ch-1 space)
ch sp(s)	chain space(s)
cl(s)	cluster(s)
cm	centimeter(s)
dc	double crochet (singular/plural)
dc dec	double crochet 2 or more stitches together, as indicated
dec	decrease/decreases/decreasing
dtr	double treble crochet
ext	extended
fpdc	front post double crochet
fpsc	front post single crochet
fptr	front post treble crochet
g	gram(s)
hdc	half double crochet
hdc dec	half double crochet 2 or more stitches together, as indicated
inc	increase/increases/increasing
lp(s)	loop(s)
MC	main color
mm	millimeter(s)
oz	ounce(s)
pc	popcorn(s)
rem	remain/remains/remaining
rep(s)	repeat(s)
rnd(s)	round(s)
RS	right side
sc	single crochet (singular/plural)
sc dec	single crochet 2 or more stitches together, as indicated
sk	skip/skipped/skipping
sl st(s)	slip stitch(es)
sp(s)	space/spaces/spaced
st(s)	stitch(es)
tog	together
tr	treble crochet
trtr	triple treble
WS	wrong side
yd(s)	yard(s)
yo	yarn over

Chain—ch: Yo, pull through lp on hook.

Slip stitch—sl st: Insert hook in st, pull through both lps on hook.

Single crochet—sc: Insert hook in st, yo, pull through st, yo, pull through both lps on hook.

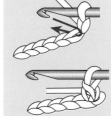

Front post stitch—fp: Back post stitch—bp: When working post st, insert hook from right to left around post st on previous row.

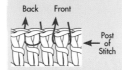

Front loop—front lp Back loop—back lp

Front Loop   Back Loop

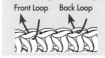

Half double crochet—hdc: Yo, insert hook in st, yo, pull through st, yo, pull through all 3 lps on hook.

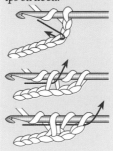

Double crochet—dc: Yo, insert hook in st, yo, pull through st, [yo, pull through 2 lps] twice.

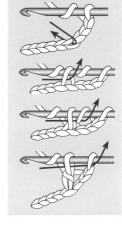

Change colors: Drop first color; with 2nd color, pull through last 2 lps of st.

Treble crochet—tr: Yo twice, insert hook in st, yo, pull through st, [yo, pull through 2 lps] 3 times.

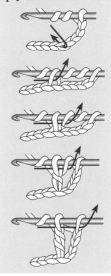

Double treble crochet—dtr: Yo 3 times, insert hook in st, yo, pull through st, [yo, pull through 2 lps] 4 times.

Single crochet decrease (sc dec): (Insert hook, yo, draw lp through) in each of the sts indicated, yo, draw through all lps on hook.

Example of 2-sc dec

Half double crochet decrease (hdc dec): (Yo, insert hook, yo, draw lp through) in each of the sts indicated, yo, draw through all lps on hook.

Example of 2-hdc dec

Double crochet decrease (dc dec): (Yo, insert hook, yo, draw loop through, draw through 2 lps on hook) in each of the sts indicated, yo, draw through all lps on hook.

Example of 2-dc dec

Example of 2-tr dec

Treble crochet decrease (tr dec): Holding back last lp of each st, tr in each of the sts indicated, yo, pull through all lps on hook.

US		UK
sl st (slip stitch)	=	sc (single crochet)
sc (single crochet)	=	dc (double crochet)
hdc (half double crochet)	=	htr (half treble crochet)
dc (double crochet)	=	tr (treble crochet)
tr (treble crochet)	=	dtr (double treble crochet)
dtr (double treble crochet)	=	ttr (triple treble crochet)
skip	=	miss

Metric
Conversion
Charts

METRIC CONVERSIONS

yards	x	.9144	=	metres (m)
yards	x	91.44	=	centimetres (cm)
inches	x	2.54	=	centimetres (cm)
inches	x	25.40	=	millimetres (mm)
inches	x	.0254	=	metres (m)

centimetres	x	.3937	=	inches
metres	x	1.0936	=	yards

INCHES INTO MILLIMETRES & CENTIMETRES (Rounded off slightly)

inches	mm	cm	inches	cm	inches	cm	inches	cm
1/8	3	0.3	5	12.5	21	53.5	38	96.5
1/4	6	0.6	5 1/2	14	22	56	39	99
3/8	10	1	6	15	23	58.5	40	101.5
1/2	13	1.3	7	18	24	61	41	104
5/8	15	1.5	8	20.5	25	63.5	42	106.5
3/4	20	2	9	23	26	66	43	109
7/8	22	2.2	10	25.5	27	68.5	44	112
1	25	2.5	11	28	28	71	45	114.5
1 1/4	32	3.2	12	30.5	29	73.5	46	117
1 1/2	38	3.8	13	33	30	76	47	119.5
1 3/4	45	4.5	14	35.5	31	79	48	122
2	50	5	15	38	32	81.5	49	124.5
2 1/2	65	6.5	16	40.5	33	84	50	127
3	75	7.5	17	43	34	86.5		
3 1/2	90	9	18	46	35	89		
4	100	10	19	48.5	36	91.5		
4 1/2	115	11.5	20	51	37	94		

KNITTING NEEDLES CONVERSION CHART

Canada/U.S.	0	1	2	3	4	5	6	7	8	9	10	10½	11	13	15
Metric (mm)	2	2¼	2¾	3¼	3½	3¾	4	4½	5	5½	6	6½	8	9	10

CROCHET HOOKS CONVERSION CHART

Canada/U.S.	1/B	2/C	3/D	4/E	5/F	6/G	8/H	9/I	10/J	10½/K	N
Metric (mm)	2.25	2.75	3.25	3.5	3.75	4.25	5	5.5	6	6.5	9.0

Itty Bitty Animals is published by DRG, 306 East Parr Road, Berne, IN 46711. Printed in USA. Copyright © 2009 DRG.
All rights reserved. This publication may not be reproduced in part or in whole without written permission from the publisher.

RETAIL STORES: If you would like to carry this pattern book or any other DRG publications, visit DRGwholesale.com.

Every effort has been made to ensure that the instructions in this publication are complete and accurate.
We cannot, however, take responsibility for human error, typographical mistakes or variations in individual work.
Please visit AnniesCustomerCare.com to check for pattern updates.

ISBN: 978-1-59635-251-3

7 8 9 10 11